San bombazo

DR. MORBITO & 1000CHANGOS

Artwork : Dainippon Type Organization

BALONY CUP 2003   ENTRÉE GRATUITE
BAR SUR PLACE

THIS
IS
NO
OFFENCE

SAMEDILE 24-05-2003
DOORS OPEN : 12H00
KICK OFF : 13H00
FINAL : 18H30

AVEC :
FC MAGNET MITTE BERLIN
WADTEAM
FG ELECTRONIC SOCCER
MISSILE
BATOFAR
AC BALONY
DJS DE CHAQUEÉ QUPE :
DIXON (SONARKOLLEKTIV, BERLIN)
STEVEN REDANT
BLUE DOG (RADIO FG)
P-O, MISTER J. & DULLABEL (MISSIVE)
GWEN MAZE (BATOFAR)
JOSS DANJEAN (BALONY)
CONTACT : BRICE@BALONYMEDIA.COM
ARTWORK : 123BUERO // TINO GRIESER

BALONY CUP 2003   GRATUITE
PLACE

THIS
IS
NO
COMPETITION

SAMEDILE 24-05-20
DOORS OPEN : 12H00
KICK OFF : 13H00
FINAL : 18H30

AVEC :
FC MAGNET MITTE BERLIN
WADTEAM
FG ELECTRONIC SOCCER
MISSILE
BATOFAR
AC BALONY
DJS DE CHAQUEÉ QUPE :
DIXON (SONARKOLLEKTIV, BERLIN)
STEVEN REDANT (FEAD)
BLUE DOG (RADIO FG)
P-O, MISTER J. & DULLABEL (MISSIVE)
GWEN MAZE (BATOFAR)
JOSS DANJEAN (BALONY)
CONTACT : BRICE@BALONYMEDIA.COM
ARTWORK : 123BUERO // TINO GRIESER

BALONY CUP 2003   GRATUITE

THIS
IS
NO
AWARD

SAMEDILE 24-05
DOORS OPEN : 13H
KICK OFF : 13H
FINAL : 18H30

AVEC :
FC MAGNET MITTE BERLIN
WADTEAM
FG ELECTRONIC SOCCER
MISSILE
BATOFAR
AC BALONY
DJS DE CHAQUEÉ QUPE :
DIXON (SONARKOLLEKTIV, BERLIN)
STEVEN REDANT
BLUE DOG
P-O, MISTER J. & DULLABES (MISSIVE)
GWEN MAZE (BATOFAR)
JOSS DANJEAN (BALONY)
CONTACT : BRICE@BALONYMEDIA.COM
ARTWORK : 123BUERO // TINO GRIESER

ENGL AND

ANPFIFF
Kick off

EASIER SAID THAN DONE?
The "Learn German" campaign is funded by German Life and Letters (GLL), the Conference of University Teachers of German in Great Britain & Ireland (CUTG), the German Academic Exchange Service (DAAD), the Goethe-Institut, IIK and Irish German Departments and Women in German Studies (WIGS). For more information on how to learn German ask your teacher, or visit http://london.daad.de, www.goethe.de/london or www.the-voyage.com/learngerman
© Concept and Design by Brighten the Corners www.brightenthecorners.com

BECK HAM

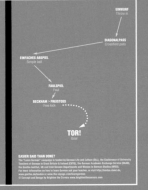

TER RY

LAMP ARD

COLE

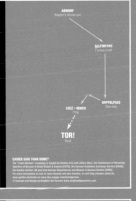

KING

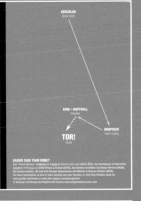

ROON EY

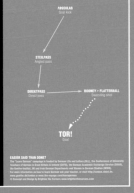

NEVI LLE

FERDI NAND

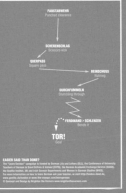

GERR ARD

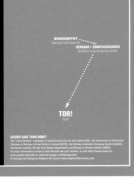

ROBI NSON

OWEN

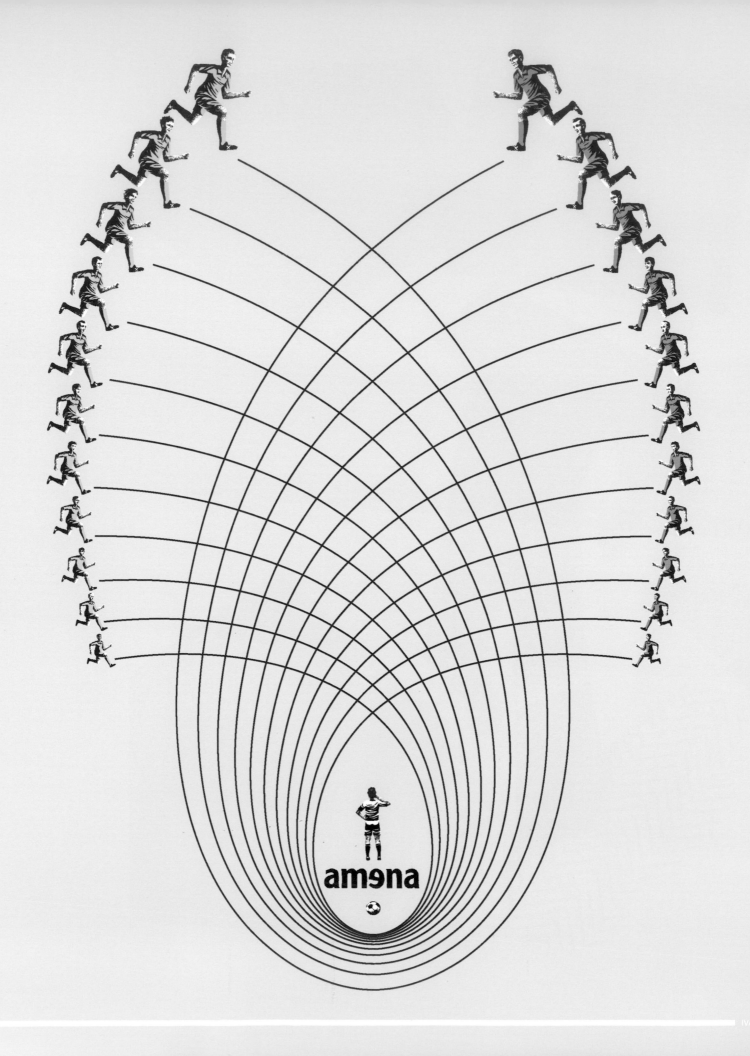

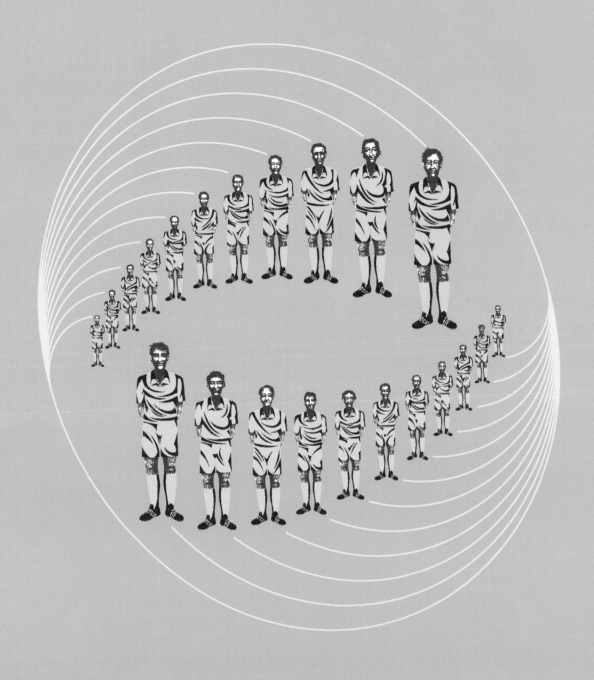

amena

PLAY
LOUD!

Comentarista
（コメンタリスタ）
マリーニョ

BRASIL

Guarda-Costas
（グアルダ コスタス）
ルッキオ / DF

Canhão
（カンニャウ）
ロベルト・カルロス / DF

Geladeira
（ジェラデイラ）
ジダ / GK

Carregador de Pianoň
（カヘガドー ヂ ピアノ）
エメルソン / MF

Guarda-Costas
（グアルダ コスタス）
ルシオ / DF

Ioiô
（ヨーヨー）
カフー / DF

HIDEAKI HOMIYAMA [TGB DESIGN.]

Roberto Carlos
¿Humildad? A ti también
Afeítate como
Beckham
Quiero a Daniella
Ronald

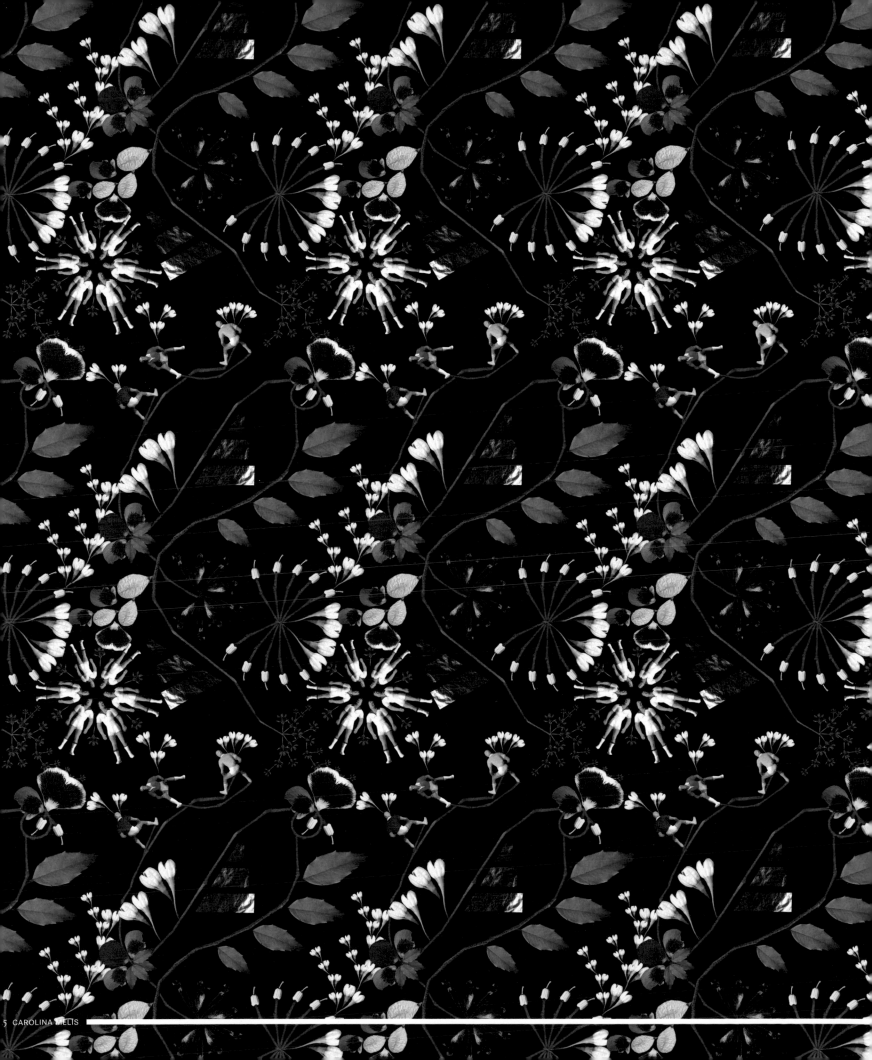

hooligan united
Brawls
Booze
&
Bicycle Kicks

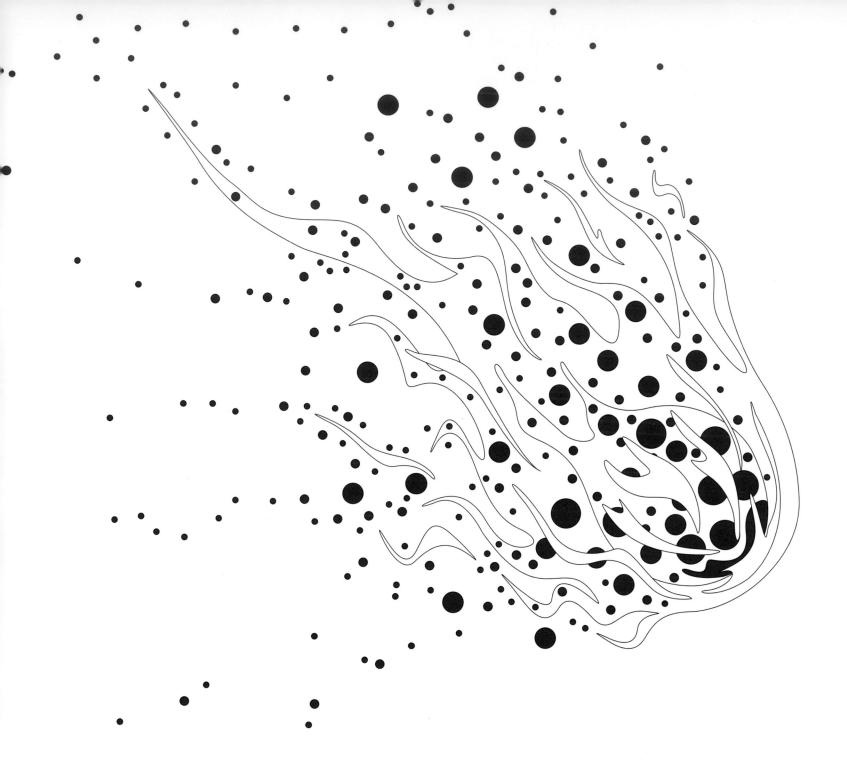

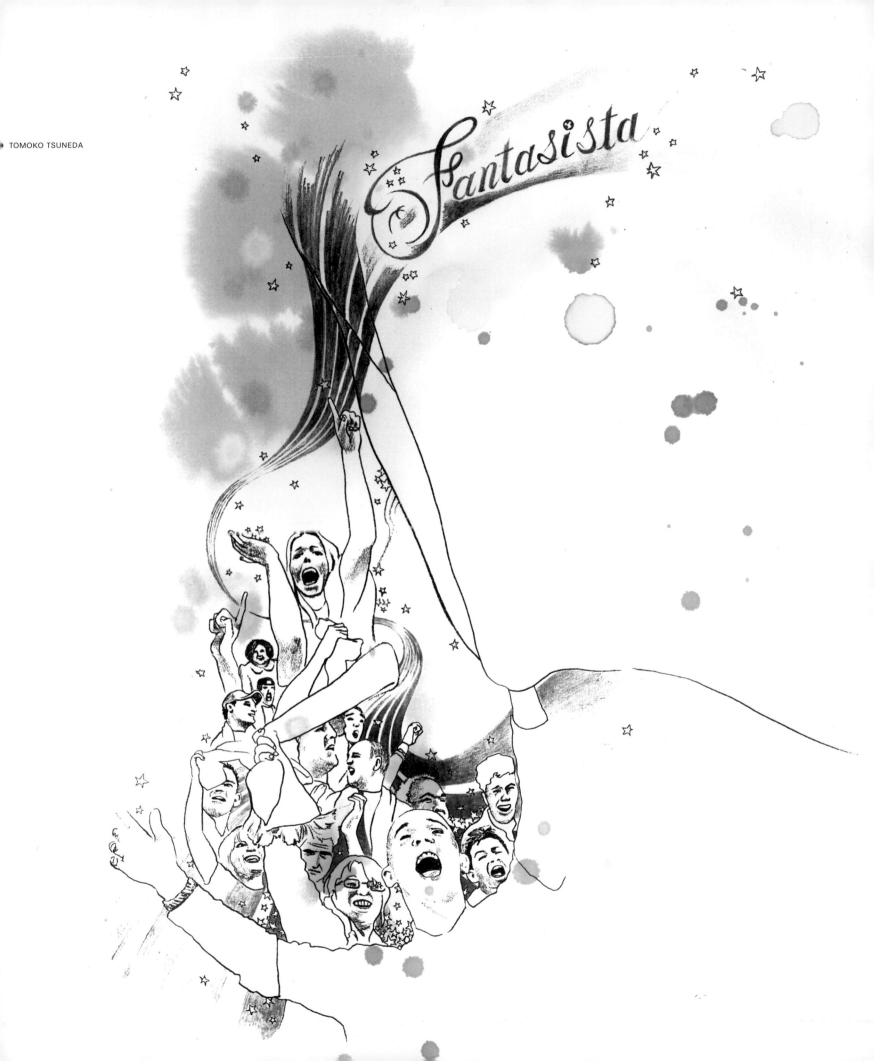

01. CHIQUITICO DURÁN

02. PATA E'PALO GÓMEZ

03. EL CALVO MIRANDA

0 6

04. EL POLLO LÓPEZ

05. BACALAO HERNÁNDEZ

07. PELUO TORRES

08. NENON FLORES

09

10

11

12. ADRIANO PENSÓN

SELECCIÓN
UCHIRE 2006

show me your tits !

HAVE IT

46.05

46.05

7

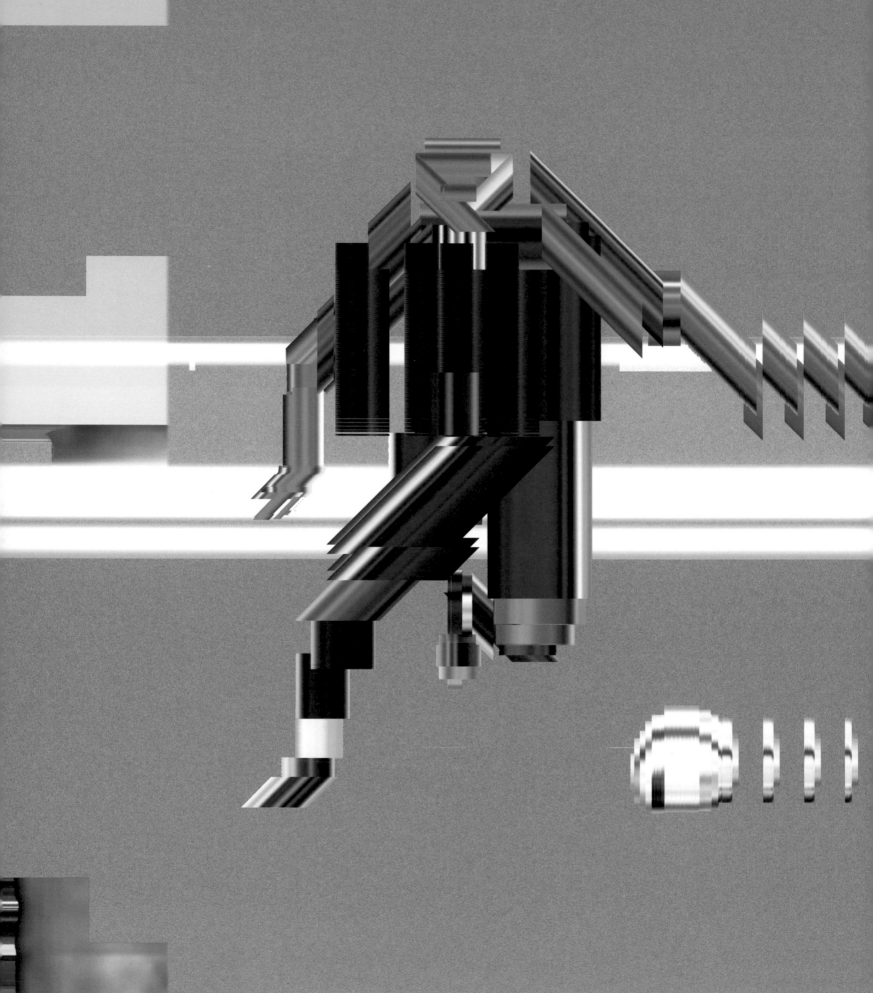

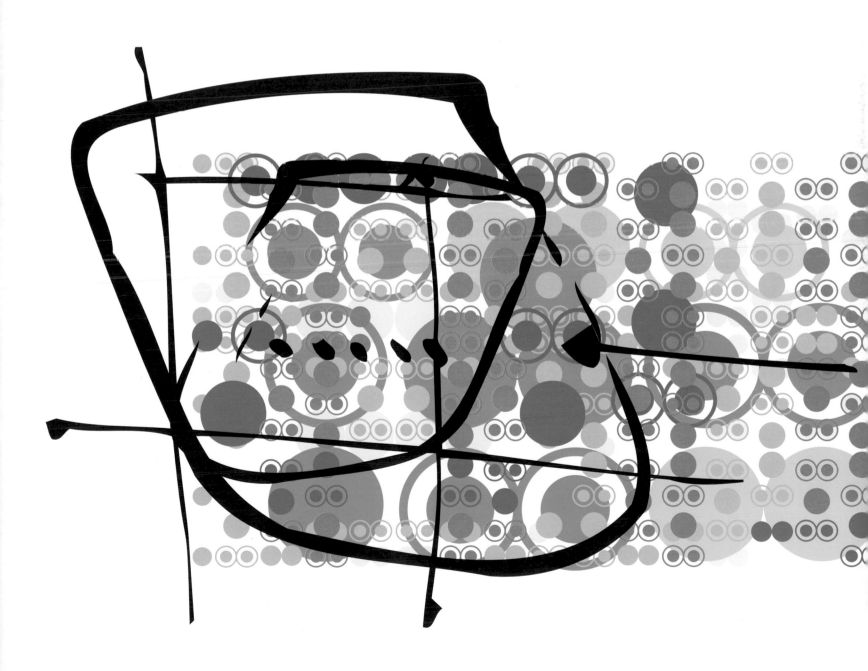

PLAY LOUD

DR. ALDERETE

Passive ©

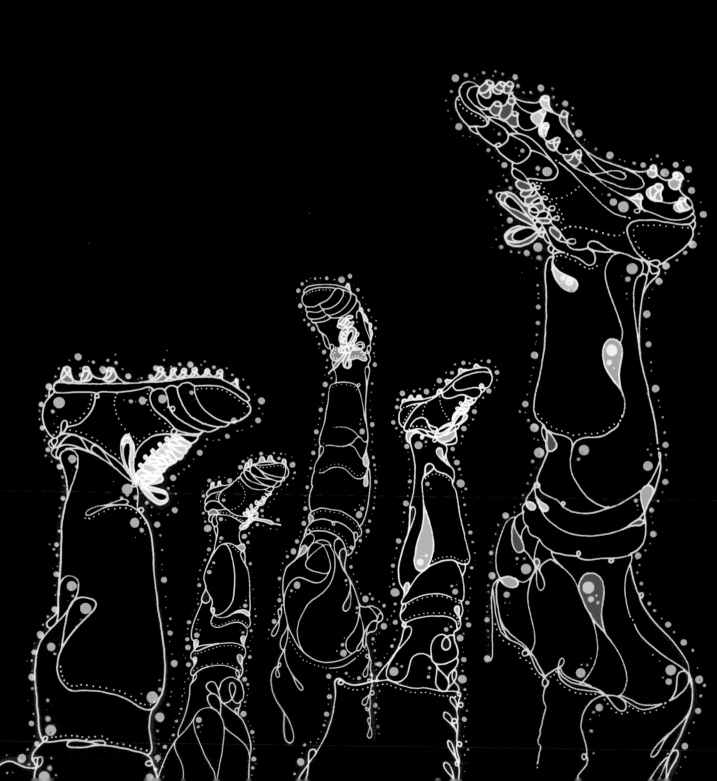

THERAPYPAREHT

BOOST2008

2006

★ KANARDO FUTBAL TEAM ★

NORA AL MANSUR

N°10

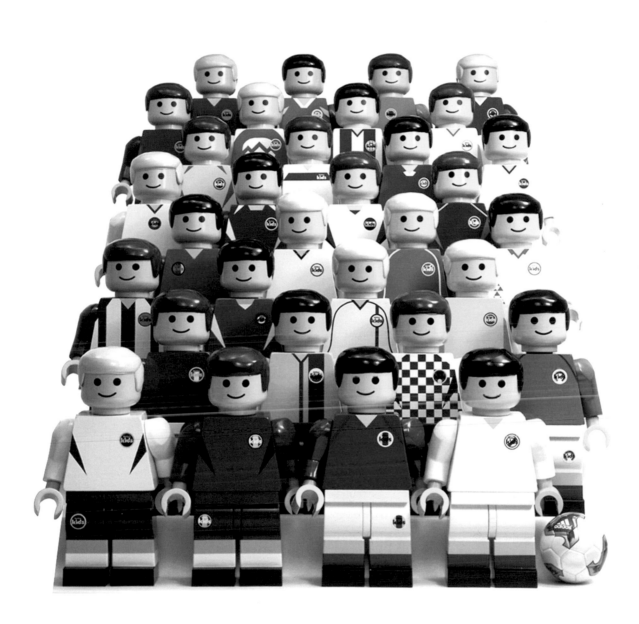

tokidoki

©2005 Simone Legno and TOKIDOKI LLC

love soccer

latte latte

tokidoki

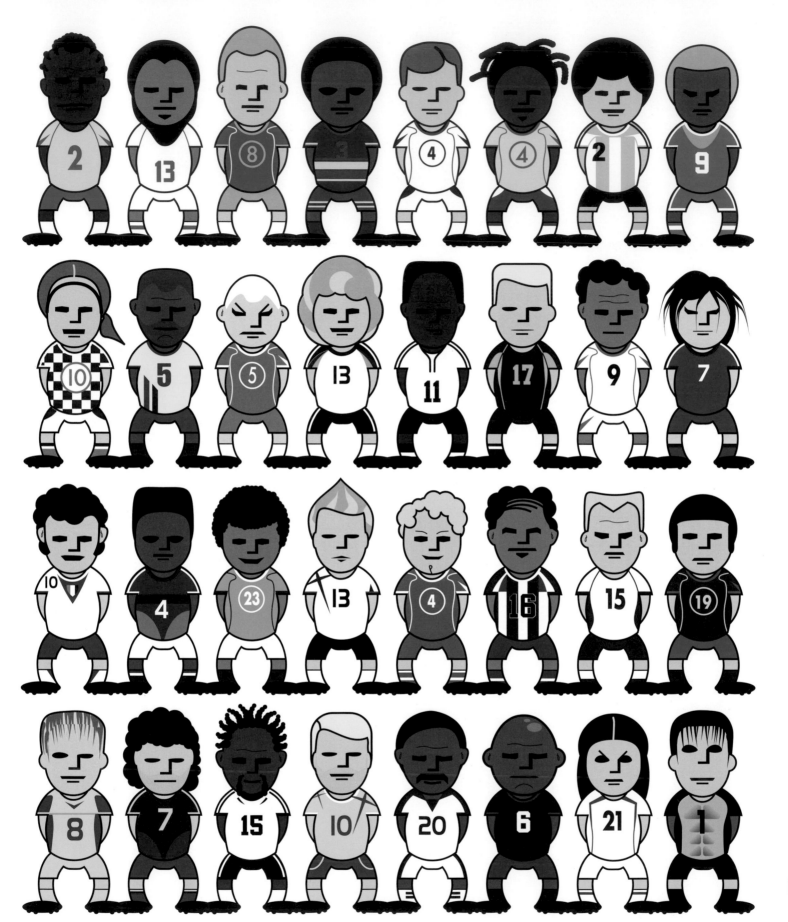

GERMANIA
2006
MONDIALI DI CALCIO
32 PAESI QUALIFICATI

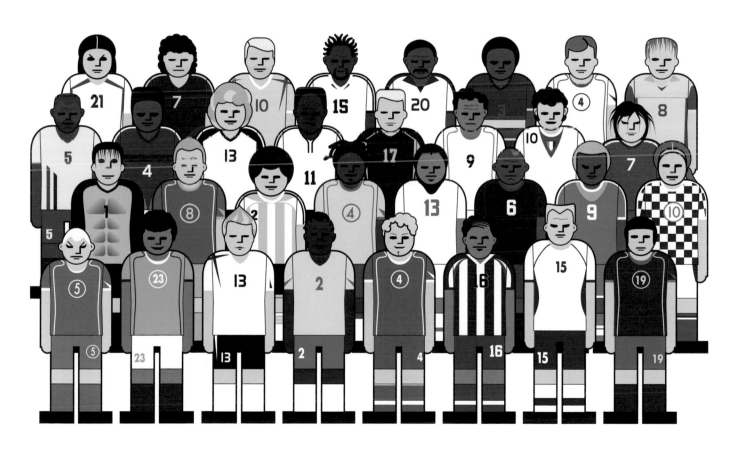

 ANG ARG AUS BRA CRC CIV CRO CZE ECU ENG FRA GER GHA IRN ITA JPN

 KOR MEX NED PAR POL POR KSA SCG ESP SWE SUI TOG TRI TUN UKR USA

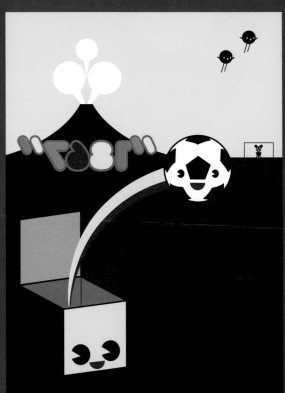

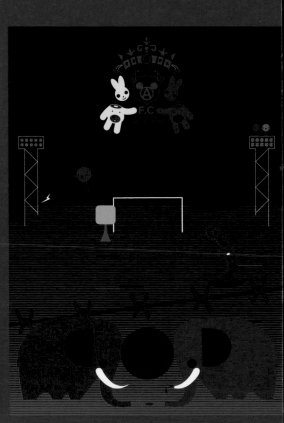

PASOaPASO

A la hora del recreo,

compra 2 potes de jugo y bébetelos

MATERIALES

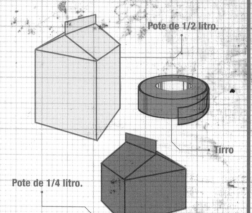

Pote de 1/2 litro.

Tirro

Pote de 1/4 litro.

A

B ARMA TU PELOTA SIGUIENDO LAS INSTRUCCIONES

1
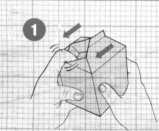
Abre el pote de 1/2 litro por la parte superior.

2
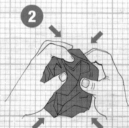
Compacta el pote de 1/4 de litro.

3
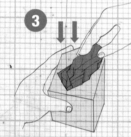
Mete el pote de 1/4 de litro dentro del pote de 1/2 litro.

4
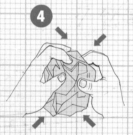
Compacta el pote de 1/2 litro.

5
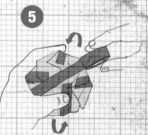
Envuelve con tirro el pote de 1/2 litro.

C

PORTERÍA

10 pasos

RECICLA

DILE NO A LAS DROGAS
patrocinado por: anónimo studio

ANÓNIMO STUDIO

NO PRACTIQUEMOS EL DEPORTE ASI

ESCOBAS

GOL EN CONTRA

MY BOLTON
BY MR OBASI

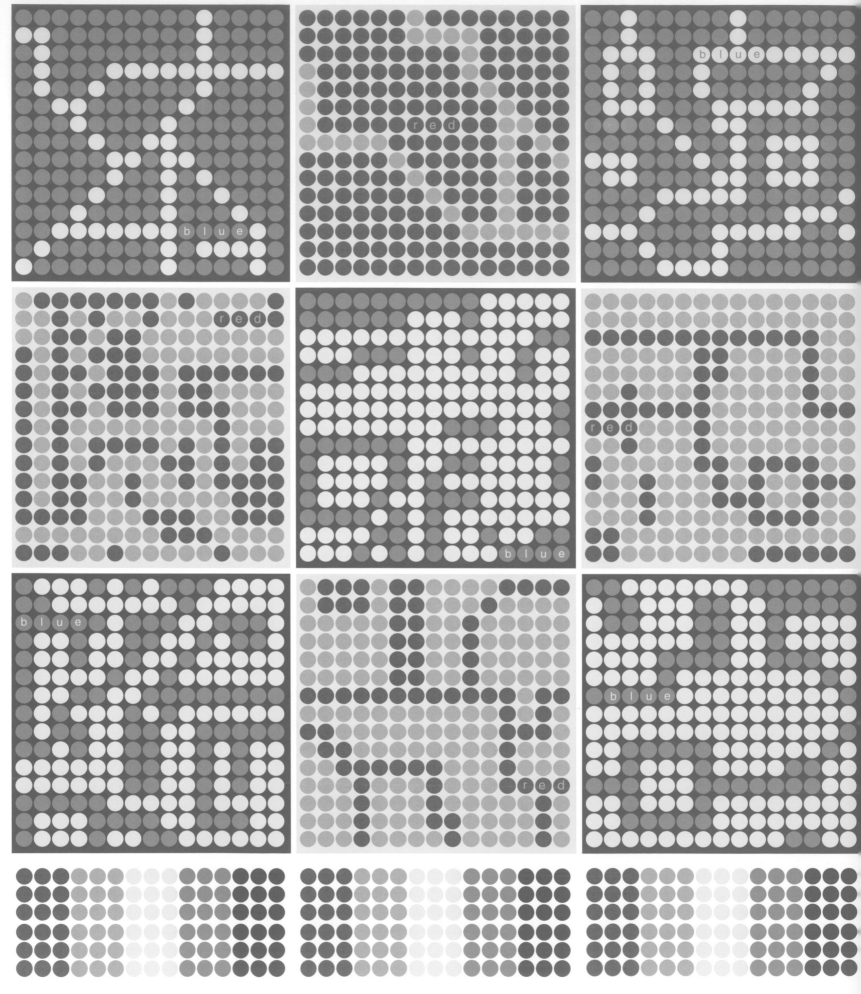

Name: Pantiestudio
Country: Mexico
www.pantiestudio.com
contacto@pantiestudio.com

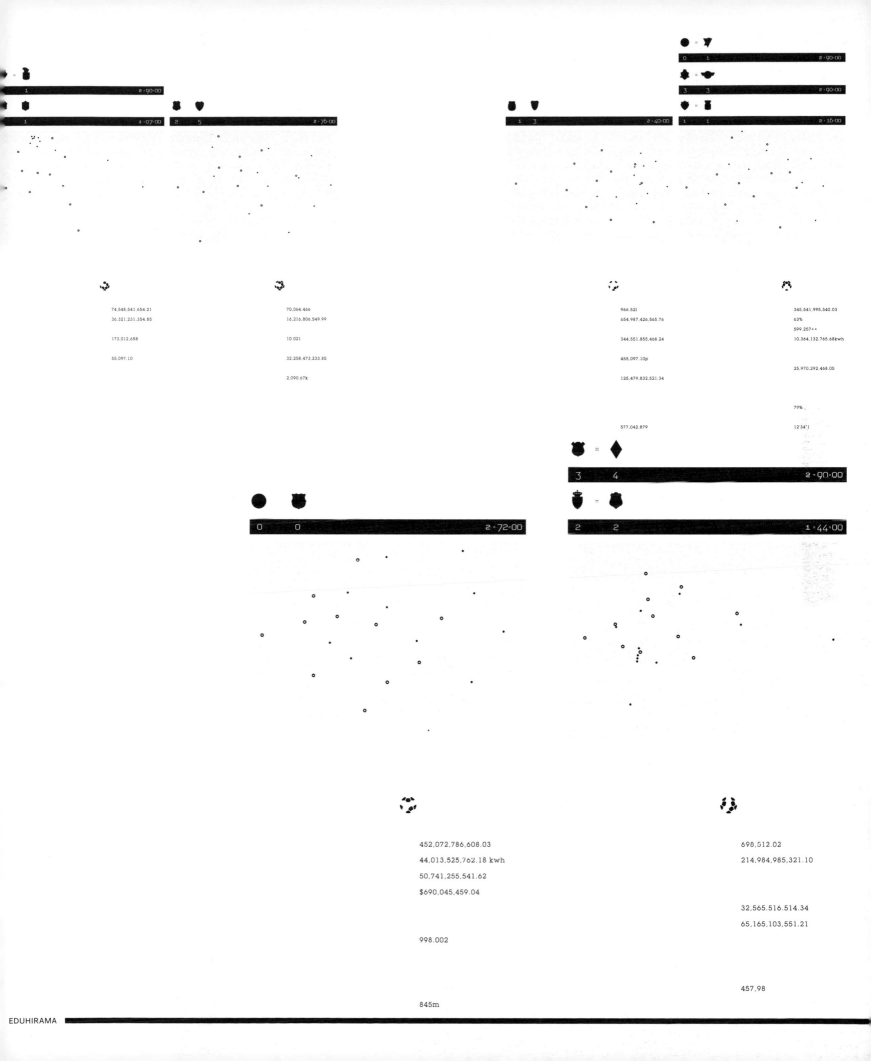

Rand van strafschopgebied / ST. JAMES PARK, Newcastle

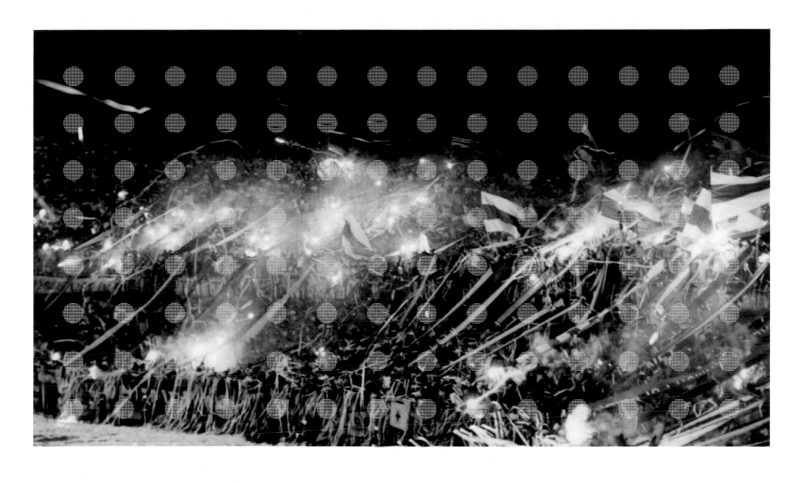

Cada noche, cada día, entre lluvias y alegrías, luchando con policías.
Yo quiero morir junto a vos campeón
Solo por vos campeón, desborda mi pasión
La razón que hay en mi existir, le encontré junto a vos.
Domingo en la mañana salgo desde el barri o vengo con los perreros a hacer fiesta en el Atanasio, el *verde* es sentimiento que se
lleva por dentro y aunque ganes o pierdas todo este pueblo sigue de fiesta, vamos, vamos...vamos vamos verde no le falles
va tu hinchada por que siempre te alentamos por que nunca te fallamos te seguimos donde vayas
Y cada avalancha,
es un sentimiento en mi corazón,
dame una alegría,
quiero verte otra vez campeón!

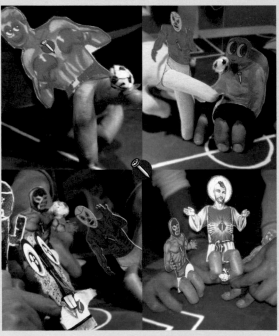

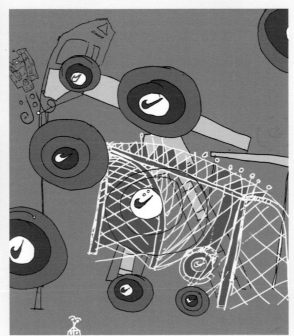

FUTBOLTECATL · AZTEC GOD OF SOCCER · DIOS AZTECA DEL FUTBOL · IN PAMBOLTEOTL IN AZTECATL · IV PAMBOLTEOTL

Mexicahuehueteotzin: Kimera mitzmomaquilitzinoa inin tlacuilolli, inin amoxtli
Un homenaje a los antiguos dioses mexicas por Gabriel Martínez Meave | A tribute to the ancient Aztec gods by Gabriel Martínez Meave

www.kimera.com.mx

George Best
Soccer player 1946-2005

Zinedine Zidane
Milieu de terrain 1972

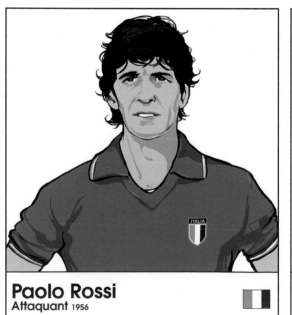

Paolo Rossi
Attaquant 1956

Michel Platini
Milieu de terrain 1955

Ronaldo
Attaquant 1976

MONDIAL 2006

UN GUIDE POUR LES JEUNES PASSIONNES DE FOOT

MATTHIEU BONNAMY   CHERIF GHEMMOUR
NASSER MABROUK   FLORIAN SANCHEZ
PIERRE-ETIENNE MINONZIO

ILLUSTRATIONS DE STEPHANE MANEL

Le baron perché

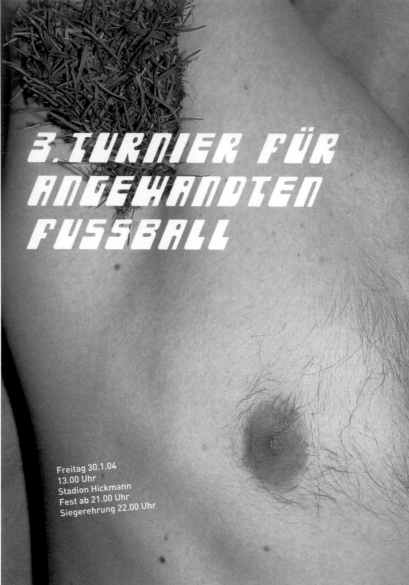

3.TURNIER FÜR
ANGEWANDTEN
FUSSBALL

Freitag 30.1.04
13.00 Uhr
Stadion Hickmann
Fest ab 21.00 Uhr
Siegerehrung 22.00 Uhr

UDENFOR SÆSONEN

Kløvermarkens idrætsanlæg | Kunstgræsbanen | Vinteren 2005-2006

ALEKSANDRA DOMANOVIC (TOP), KAROLY KIRALYFALVI (BOTTOM LEFT), CYKLON (BOTTOM RIGHT)

••• Esta es La Historia D La Tota Carbajal •••

TAMBIEN CONOCIDO COMO

"EL CINCO COPAS"

BRASIL 50 SUIZA 54 CHILE 62 SUECIA 58 INGLATERRA 66

"Jugaba con el cantante José Alfredo Jiménez, que jugaba como portero, éramos compañeros en el barrio. Aunque le importaba gorro que le metieran gol, siempre andaba en la luna y a veces ebrio con tequila"

Antonio Carbajal es el jugador mexicano con más juegos en Copa del Mundo y aunque tiene muchos goles recibidos en los Mundiales, la verdad es que sin él, o con José Alfredo Jimenez en la portería, el equipo mexicano hubiera recibido más. Por eso...

hey laydeez

En México, un gol no vale nada.

CHA³

**So 31/07/05
13:00 bis 20:00 Uhr
Stadion Festwiese**

Talstrasse 207 / 70372 Stuttgart / Eintritt 5,-

Ampulle	Prairie
Amici	Rohbau
Barcode	Rote Kapelle
Bravo Charlie	Stella Maris
Boa	San's
Come Prima	Schocken
Deli	Suite 212
Hidden Place	Scholz
Insomnia	Schlesinger
Love Academy	Soho
Oggi	Waranga
Perkins Park	Zotti/Barista

GASTRO CUP 05

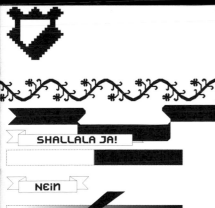

SHALLALA JA!

NEiN

JAAA!

FC SCHWAEBISCH HALL
FV KIEL
KARLSRUHE SC
FC OFFENBURG

NEEE!

HERTHA BSC

BAYERN MUENCHEN

2098 ©

BETREFF:
04.08.2001
NEU!

HTTP://WWW.ZWE
ITAUSENDACHTU
NDNEUNZIG.DE

SEHR GEEHRTE DAMEN UND HERREN

ERNSTHAFTE VERSUCHE, DENKENDE MASCHINEN ZU BAUEN, SETZTEN NACH DEM ZWEITEN WELTKRIEG EIN. EINE FORSCHUNGSRICHTUNG, KYBERNETIK GENANNT, VERWENDETE ELEKTRONISCHE SCHALTKREISE, DIE DAS NERVENSYSTEM INITIIERTEN, UM MASCHINEN ZU KONSTRUIEREN, DIE EINFACHE MUSTER ZU ERKENNEN LERNTEN, ODER UM SCHILDKRÖTENARTIGE ROBOTER ZU BAUEN, DIE IHREN WEG ZUR AUFLADESTATION FANDEN. EIN ANDERER ANSATZ, KÜNSTLICHE INTELLIGENZ GENANNT, VERWENDETE DIE ARITHMETISCHE LEISTUNG DER NACHKRIEGSCOMPUTER ZUM ABSTRAKTEN SCHLU FOLGERN UND STELLTE WÄHREND DER 60ER JAHRE COMPUTER HER, DIE LOGISCHE UND GEOMETRISCHE THEOREME BEWIESEN, RECHENPROBLEME LÖSTEN UND GUTE SCHACHSPIELE AUSFÜHREN KONNTEN. ENDE DER 60ER JAHRE VERBANDEN FORSCHERTEAMS AM MIT UND IN STANFORD IHRE COMPUTER MIT FERNSEHKAMERAS UND ROBOTERARMEN, WODURCH DENKENDE PROGRAMME BEGINNEN KONNTEN, INFORMATIONEN DIREKT VON DER ÄU EREN WELT AUFZUNEHMEN.

MIT FREUNDLICHEN GRUESSEN

5 WEKEN WK
VOOR 25 GULDEN.

Het PAROOL

5 WEKEN WK
VOOR 25 GULDEN.

Het PAROOL

5 WEKEN WK
VOOR 25 GULDEN.

Het PAROOL

5 WEKEN WK
VOOR 25 GULDEN.

Het PAROOL

Nieuw.
Hard Gras no. 14

THEO VAN DE BURCH

VERDEDIGER, F.C. DEN HAAG/A.D.O. Geboren: 15-11-'43. Theo van de Burch is een sterke rechtsverdediger, die in een wedstrijd tot een grootse vorm kan groeien. Van de Burch schrikt er ook niet voor terug om mee aan te vallen.

THEO VAN DE BURCH

TAPIJTGIGANT, RIJSWIJK Geboren: 15-11-'43. Theo van de Burch is een sterke directeur, die tegenwoordig alleen nog tapijt neerlegt. Van de Burch schrikt er niet van terug om hier met z'n favoriete monster te poseren.

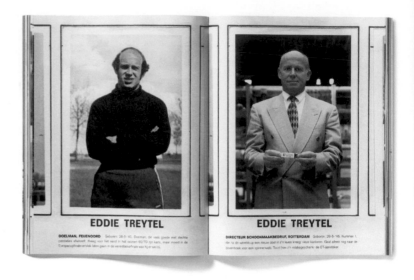

EDDIE TREYTEL

DOELMAN, FEIJENOORD Geboren: 28-5-'46. Doelman, die veelk goede met slechte prestaties afwisselt. Kreeg voor het eerst in het seizoen 69/70 zijn kans, maar moest in de Europacupfinalewedstrijk laten zien in de wereldklasftrije was hij er wel bij.

EDDIE TREYTEL

DIRECTEUR SCHOONMAAKBEDRIJF, ROTTERDAM Geboren: 28-5-'46. Nummer 1, de na de wereldcup een nieuwe deel in z'n leven kreeg: vloer kantoren. Gaat alleen nog naar de bovenkast voor een opmerkweb. Toont hier z'n middaggeschenk: de ET-sprotoken.

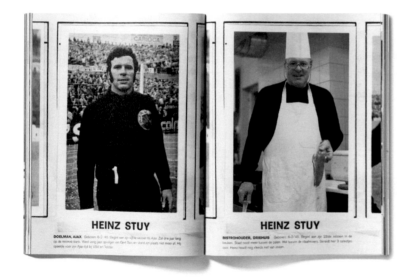

HEINZ STUY

DOELMAN, AJAX Geboren: 6-2-'45. Begint van op-z'll-e vezer to Ajax. Zal drie jaar lang op de reserve-bank. Vond ung jaar opvolger om Gert Bals en stond zijn plaats niet meer af. Hij speelde voor zijn Ajax-tijd bij VSV en Telstar.

HEINZ STUY

BISTROHOUDER, DRIEHUIS Geboren: 6-2-'45. Begint aan zijn 22ste: reizen in de keuken. Staat nooit meer tussen de palen. Wel tussen de vitaalmixers. Streedt hier 3 cateltjes voor. Heeg houdt nog steeds niet van vissen.

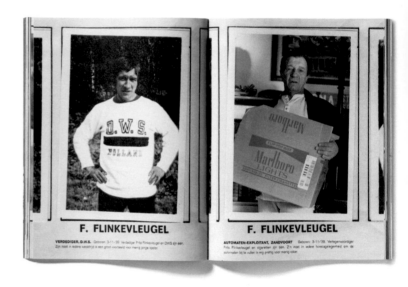

F. FLINKEVLEUGEL

VERDEDIGER, D.W.S. Geboren: 3-11-'35. Verdediger Frits Flinkevleugel en DWS zijn een. Zijn inzet in iedere wedstrijd is een groot voorbeeld voor menig jonge speler.

F. FLINKEVLEUGEL

AUTOMATEN-EXPLOITANT, ZANDVOORT Geboren: 3-11-'35. Vertegenwoordiger Frits Flinkevleugel en sigaretten zijn één. Zijn inzet in iedere horecagelegenheid om de automaten bij te vullen is erg prettig voor menig roker.

ANELIDE TOFANI
UIT DE

IGOR FRANCE
UIT DE PIJP

VIOLA OLEVIA ARNON
UIT OOST

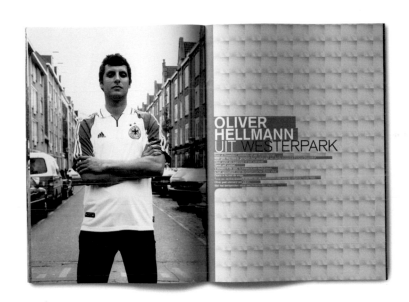

OLIVER HELLMANN
UIT WESTERPARK

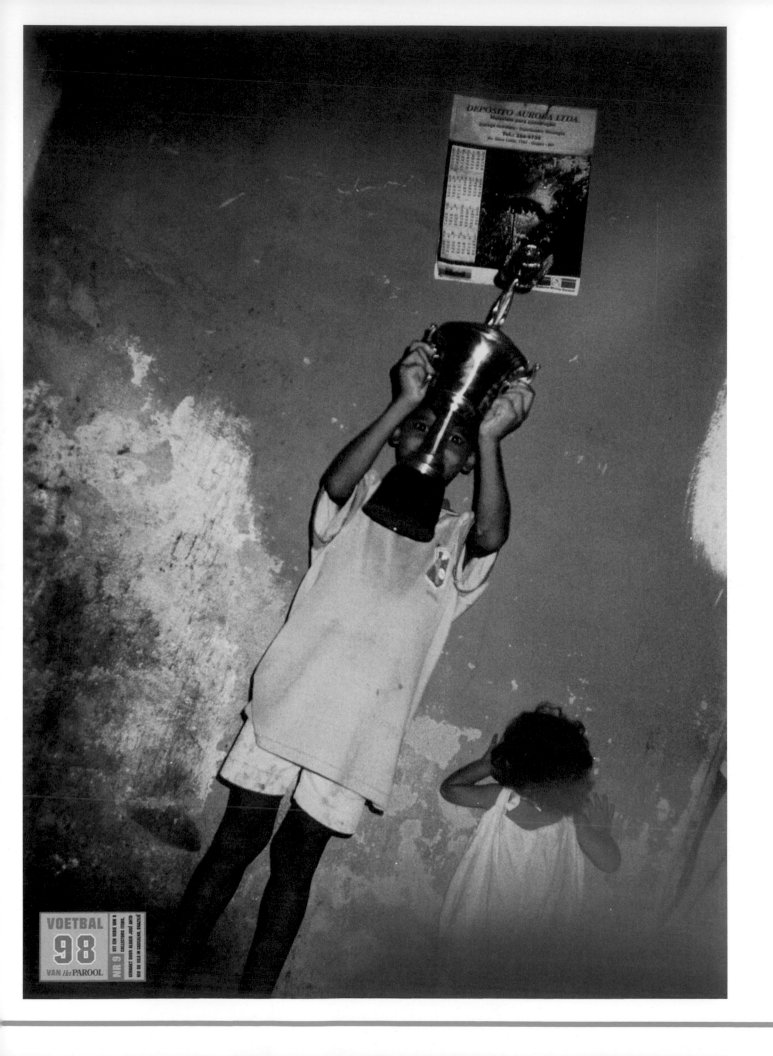

Plymouth, former capital

Rose Willock, Family radio

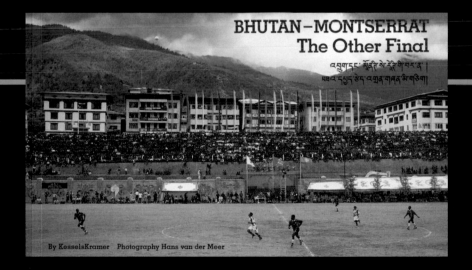

BHUTAN–MONTSERRAT
The Other Final

འབྲུག་དང་མོན་ཊི་སེ་རཊ་ཀྱི་བར་ན།
མཐའ་འཁྱུད་ཆེན་འགྲན་བསྡུར་གནང་མི་ཅི།

By KesselsKramer   Photography Hans van der Meer

1:0 4th minute.

3D SOCCER MODELING KIT

3D SOCCER MODELING KIT

3D SOCCER MODELING KIT

KEL
Jazzy Deportistas presents

Football is Beautiful

Fußball
Jünkie

Fußball
Vergiftung

Fußball
Jünkie

ROCKGOL 2006

 Football Font

MAKAAY

SMOLAREK

FIGO

TOTTI

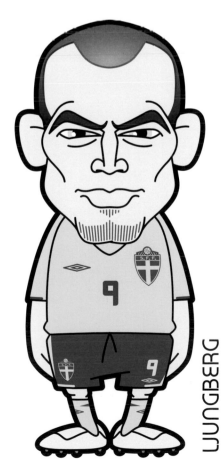

LJUNGBERG

TAKAHARA

NEDVED

CRESPO

SANTA CRUZ

BALLACK

DROGBA

DONOVAN

SHEVCHENKO

RONALDINHO

ZIDANE

BECKHAM

RAUL

KAHN

MARQUEZ

FC WALVISCH

FC WALVISCH

FC WALVISCH

FC WALVISCH

FC WALVISCH

FC WALVISCH

FC WALVISCH

FC WALVISCH

FC WALVISCH

FC WALVISCH

FC WALVISCH

FC WALVISCH

FC WALVISCH

FC WALVISCH

FC WALVISCH

Home Jersey

Away Jersey

Supporter T-shirt

Game short

Socks

Innershirt

Knit Beanie

Wallet

Bucket hat

Coaching Board

Supporter's Scarf

Captain's Armband

Stretcher

Shinguard

Shoe Bag

Game Duffle   side

Mug

VIAGRAFIK
SPORT-BRANDING™

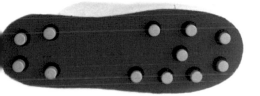

MAILAND ODER MADRID
HAUPTSACHE
ITALIEN

ANDY MÖLLER

DAS WIRD ALLES VON DEN
MEDIEN
HOCHSTERILISIERT

BRUNO LABBADIA

TURNIER FÜR ANGEWANDTEN FUSSBALL
1.FEB/ab 13.00

DAS HABE ICH IHM DANN AUCH
VERBAL GESAGT
MARIO BASLER

ICH BIN KÖRPERLICH
UND PHYSISCH
TOPFIT
THOMAS HÄSSLER

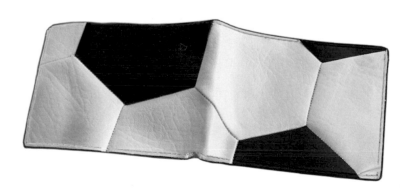

PLAYER: 123BUERO | TIMO GAESSNER
TEAM: GERMANY
WWW.123BUERO.COM • HELLO@123BUERO.COM
123BUERO – GRAPHIC DESIGN STUDIO. FOCUSED ON CONSULTING,
TYPOGRAPHY, PRINT & IMAGE.
NUMBER: 6
CLIENT: BALCONY MAGAZIN • YEAR: 2003

PLAYER: 2098
TEAM: GERMANY
WWW.2098.ORG • INFO@2098.ORG
NUMBER: 100, 101
CLIENT: PERSONAL WORK • YEAR: 2001 • DESIGNERS: THOMAS
EBERWEIN, RALPH HEINSOHN, MARTIN HESSELMEIER, HANSGEORG
SCHWARZ • INFO: FOOTBALL TEAMS AND THEIR FANS SHARE VERY
STRONG VISUAL IDENTITIES ALMOST LIKE CIS IN GRAPHIC DESIGN.
AT THAT TIME WE DEVELOPED A CI FOR OUR DESIGN COLLECTIVE
AND DID CHOOSE FOOTBALL AS A WAY TO PRESENT IT IN CONTEXT.

PLAYER: 3 DELUXE
TEAM: GERMANY
WWW.3DELUXE.DE
NUMBER: 42
CLIENT: PERSONAL WORK • YEAR: 2005 • INFOS: GIVEAWAY ARTICLE
FOR 3DELUXE CLIENTS
NUMBER: 43
CLIENT: PERSONAL WORK • YEAR: 2005 • INFOS: KEYVISUAL ZUM
KUNST- UND KULTURPROGRAMM DER BUNDESREGIERUNG ZUR FIFA
WM 2006TM
NUMBER: 60
CLIENT: PERSONAL WORK • YEAR: 2005

PLAYER: ACAMPANTE
TEAM: ARGENTINA
WWW.MIACAMPANTE.COM • SEBA@MIACAMPANTE.COM
NUMBER: 31
CLIENT: PERSONAL WORK • YEAR: 2006 • INFOS: PINGÜINO Y
PECHO FRÍO.

PLAYER: ALEKSANDRA DOMANOVIC
TEAM: AUSTRIA
WWW.KLASSEHICKMANN.COM • HTTP://DIEANGEWANDTE.AT
NUMBER: 96
CLIENT: PERSONAL WORK • YEAR: 2006 • INFOS: STUDENT PROJECT
"TURNIER FÜR ANGEWANDTEN FUSSBALL 2002" AT UNIVERSITY OF
APPLIED ARTS VIENNA, CLASS OF FONS HICKMANN; INSTALLATION
POSTER USING A BALLOON FOR THE TOURNAMENT BETWEEN 16
TEAMS, HELD IN THE LOFT OF FONS HICKMANNS CLASS AT THE UNI-
VERSITY • SUPERVISION: FONS HICKMANN, KATHARINA USCHAN

PLAYER: ANÓNIMO STUDIO
TEAM: VENEZUELA
WWW.ANONIMOSTUDIO.COM
ANONIMO@ANONIMOSTUDIO.COM
FOR SIX YEARS ANÓNIMO STUDIO HAS BEEN OFFERING GRAPHIC
DESIGN AND ANIMATION SERVICES. FROM CONCEPT TO COMPLETION,
WE PROVIDE INTEGRAL SERVICES FOR PRINT, AUDIOVISUAL AND
DIGITAL MEDIAS. ANONIMO STUDIO IS FORMED BY ALBERTO HADYAR,
JESÚS MARQUEZ, HENRY RIVERO, HECTOR DO NASCIMENTO, AROL
REYES AND DANIEL BORRAT
NUMBER: 72, 99
CLIENT: PERSONAL WORK • YEAR: 2006

PLAYER: ARNIKA MÜLL
TEAM: FRANCE
WWW.ARNIKA-MUELL.COM • INFO@ARNIKA-MUELL.COM
NUMBER: 118
CLIENT: PERSONAL WORK • YEAR: 2006 • TECHNIQUE: ACRYL-
COLORS, FINELINER, PAPER, CRAYON 30CM X 25CM

PLAYER: BANKER WESSEL
TEAM: SWEDEN
WWW.BANKERWESSEL.COM • INFO@BANKERWESSEL.COM
NUMBER: 11
CLIENT: FIFA • YEAR: 2002 • INFO: POSTER FOR FIFAWORLDCUP.COM
NUMBER: 87
CLIENT: FIFA • YEAR: 2002 • INFO: CHARACTERS FOR AN ANIMATION
AT FIFAWORLDCUP.COM

PLAYER: BENJAMIN GÜDEL
TEAM: SWITZERLAND
WWW.GUEDEL.BIZ • BENJAMIN@GUEDEL.BIZ
NUMBER: 116
CLIENT: PERSONAL WORK

PLAYER: BRIGHTEN THE CORNERS
TEAM: UNITED KINGDOM
WWW.BRIGHTENTHECORNERS.COM
CONTACT@BRIGHTENTHECORNERS.COM
CLIENT: DEUTSCHER AKADEMISCHER AUSTAUSCHDIENST (DAAD),
GOETHE-INSTITUT • YEAR: 2006 • DESIGNERS: FRANK PHILIPPIN,
BILLY KIOSSOGLOU • INFO: A SET OF 12 POSTCARDS (FRONT AND
BACK) PROMOTING GERMAN AS A LANGUAGE IN THE UK.

PLAYER: CAROLINA MELIS
TEAM: UNITED KINGDOM
WWW.CAROLINAMELIS.COM • CARO@CAROLINAMELIS.COM
NUMBER: 25
CLIENT: ROJO / ADIDAS • YEAR: 2005

PLAYER: CHA3 (FRITZ+VERDIN)
TEAM: MEXICO
REDOBA501@YAHOO.COM
CHA 3 FORMADO POR FRITZ TORRES Y JORGE VERDIN. EL TALLER
CHA3, NO ES UN ESTUDIO O DESPACHO DE DISEÑO PROPIAMENTE
DICHO, SINO MÁS BIEN UN PRETEXTO PARA REALIZAR EL TRABAJO
VISUAL A SU GUSTO, RINDIENDO HOMENAJE A LAS EXPRESIONES
VERNÁCULAS DE LA REGIÓN EN DONDE VIVEN.
NUMBER: 36
CLIENT: PERSONAL WORK • YEAR: 2006 • INFOS: FOTO DE "LA
TOTA CARBAJAL"
NUMBER: 97
CLIENT: PERSONAL WORK • YEAR: 2006

PLAYER: CHALET | FRANÇOIS CHALET
TEAM: SWITZERLAND
WWW.FRANCOISCHALET.CH • BONJOUR@FRANCOISCHALET.CH
NUMBER: 71
CLIENT: PERSONAL WORK

PLAYER: CHENNA | PPAINT
TEAM: UNITED KINGDOM
WWW.UNIT.NL • INFO@PPAINT.NET • INFO@UNIT.NL
NUMBER: 18
CLIENT: NIKE • ILLUSTRATION: CHENNA@PPAINT • YEAR: 2004 •
DESIGNER: JOHN BUTTERWORTH @ HAYMARKET PUBLICATION •
INFO: HAYMARKET PUBLICATION COMMISSIONED AN ILLUSTRATION
OF A STEP BY STEP GUIDE ON HOW TO DO THE "RONALDO STEP
OVER" FOR THE NIKE PUBLICATION "NUTMEG"

PLAYER: CHRISTOPH PRIGLINGER
TEAM: AUSTRIA
WWW.KLASSEHICKMANN.COM • HTTP://DIEANGEWANDTE.AT
NUMBER: 130, 131
CLIENT: PERSONAL WORK • YEAR: 2006 • INFOS: STUDENT PROJECT
"TURNIER FÜR ANGEWANDTEN FUSSBALL 2002" AT UNIVERSITY OF
APPLIED ARTS VIENNA, CLASS OF FONS HICKMANN; 4 OF 6 POSTERS
OF ARTIFICIAL GRAS DISPLAYING SURREAL VERBAL ACCIDENTS OF
GERMAN FOOTBALL PLAYERS FOR THE TOURNAMENT BETWEEN 16
TEAMS, HELD IN THE LOFT OF FONS HICKMANNS CLASS AT THE UNI-
VERSITY • SUPERVISION: FONS HICKMANN, KATHARINA USCHAN

PLAYER: CLAUDIA MÜLLER
TEAM: GERMANY
CIMHAMBURG@GMX.DE
NUMBER: 129
CLIENT: PERSONAL WORK • YEAR: 2005 • INFO: FOOTBALL
SLIPPERS "HOME PLAY" • MATERIAL: WOOL, LEATHER, SPIKES

PLAYER: CUARTOPISO
TEAM: COLOMBIA
WWW.CUARTOPISO.COM • ALEJO@CUARTOPISO.COM
IDENTITY, PRINT, WEB AND MOTION FOR GRAPHIC CONSCIOUS CLIENTS.
NUMBER: 83
CLIENT: PERSONAL WORK • YEAR: 2006 • DESIGNER: ALEJANDRO
POSADA

PLAYER: CYKLON
TEAM: DENMARK
WWW.CYKLONGRAFIK.NET • CYKLON@CYKLON.DK
CYKLON IS HENRIK GYTZ, INDEPENDENT GRAPHIC DESIGNER BASED
IN COPENHAGEN, DENMARK. THE COMPANY WAS INITIATED IN 2002
AFTER A ONE-YEAR WORKING PERIOD AT BÜRO DESTRUCT IN BERN,
SWITZERLAND. CYKLON IS A MULTI DISCIPLINARY STUDIO WORKING
IN THE FIELDS OF GRAPHIC DESIGN FOR PRINT, BRANDING, AND
INTERACTION DESIGN.
NUMBER: 96
CLIENT: PERSONAL WORK • YEAR: 2005 INFO: THE FORMAT IS
POST CARDS. THE PHOTOS ARE TAKEN AT THE ARTIFICIAL LAWN PIT
CLOSE TO THE STUDIO. THE WINTER-TRAINING FACILITIES BELONG TO
"KLØVERMARKEN FB" WHO PLAY IN A LOCAL COPENHAGEN LEAGUE

PLAYER: DAINIPPON TYPE ORGANIZATION
TEAM: JAPAN
HTTP://DAINIPPON.TYPE.ORG/ • DAINIPPON@TYPE.ORG
NUMBER: 4
CLIENT: NIKE JAPAN + 3WWW • YEAR: 2004

PLAYER: DED ASSOCIATES
TEAM: UNITED KINGDOM
WWW.DEDASS.COM
NUMBER: 70
CLIENT: SELF PROMOTIONAL • YEAR: 2006

PLAYER: DISCODOENER
TEAM: GERMANY
WWW.DISCODOENER.DE • INFO@DISCODOENER.DE
AGENTUR FÜR KOMUNIKATION UND DESIGN
NUMBER: 98
CLIENT: DIE ROTE KAPELLE (STUTTGART) • FOTO: SUZANA JELIC •
GRAFIK: MARCUS FISCHER, PETER PALEC, PIT LEDERLE • AGENTUR
DISCODOENER • YEAR: 2005 • DESIGNER: MARCUS FISCHER,
PETER PALEC, PIT LEDERLE)

PLAYER: DOMA
TEAM: ARGENTINA
WWW.DOMA.TV • INFLO@DOMA.TV
ILUSTRATION, ANIMATION, FILM, TOY DESIGN.
NUMBER: 68
CLIENT: PERSONAL WORK • YEAR: 2006

PLAYER: DR. ALDERETE
TEAM: MEXICO
WWW.JORGEALDERETE.COM
POP ILLUSTRATOR, USING TRASH CULTURE, 50'S SCIENCE FICTION
FILMS, WRESTLING AND SURF MUSIC IMAGERY IN HIS PSYCHOTRONIC
ILLUSTRATIONS, ANIMATIONS AND COMICS. HE HAS WORKED FOR
MTV LATIN AMERICA AND JAPAN, NICKELODEON LATIN AMERICA
AND BRAZIL. CURRENTLY HE MOSTLY WORKS AS AN ILLUSTRATOR,
FOR DIFFERENT PUBLISHING AND MEDIA VENTURES IN ARGENTINA,
MEXICO, SPAIN, ITALY, GERMANY, PORTUGAL, USA, SWITZERLAND,
FINLAND, ETC. HE WORKS IN HIS LAB AT MEXICO CITY.
NUMBER: 48
CLIENT: PERSONAL WORK • YEAR: 2005
NUMBER: 91
CLIENT: NIKE • YEAR: 2004 • INFOS: PART OF THE FOOTBALL
STREET POSTERS DOING BY HEMATOMA COLLECTIVE.

PLAYER: DR. MORBITO & 1000CHANGOS
TEAM: MEXICO
DRMORBITO@YAHOO.COM.MX, RUDA71@YAHOO.COM.MX
MORBITO ES UN WEY QUE HACE MUÑEQUITOSW, MILCHANGOS UN
WEY QUE SE AZOTA EN LAS PAREDES.
NUMBER: 3
CLIENT: PERSONAL WORK • YEAR: 2004

PLAYER: DRAGON
TEAM: JAPAN
WWW.DRAGON76.NET
NUMBER: 20 – 23
CLIENT: BUNGEISHUNJU LTD • YEAR: 2004

PLAYER: Eddymir Briceño
TEAM: Venezuela
EDDYVENE@YAHOO.ES
NUMBER: 34
CLIENT: PERSONAL WORK • YEAR: 2005 • INFO: ILUSTRACIÓN Y
CONCEPTUALIZACIÓN EDDYMIR BRICEÑO

PLAYER: Eduhirama
TEAM: Brazil
EDUHIRAMA@YAHOO.COM.BR
ILUSTRATIONS, IDENTITY & EDITORIAL DESIGN
NUMBER: 81
CLIENT: PERSONAL WORK

PLAYER: Escobas
TEAM: Mexico
WWW.ESCOBAS.COM.MX • ESCOBAS@ESCOBAS.COM.MX
AMANTE Y COLECCIONISTA DE TODA LA GRÁFICA POPULAR MEXICANA
SIENDO ESTA LA BASE DE SU TRABAJO
NUMBER: 73
CLIENT: PERSONAL WORK • YEAR: 2005 • DESIGNER: Eduardo
Escobar Beckwith

PLAYER: Fakir
TEAM: Mexico
FAKIRI@PRODIGY.NET.MX
FAKIR (1995), LABORATORIO CREATIVO QUE DESARROLLÓ LA REVISTA
FAKIR Y QUE HA REALIZADO EXPERIMENTOS EN DIVERSAS ACTIVIDADES
GRÁFICAS, VISUALES Y AUDITIVAS.
NUMBER: 84
CLIENT: PERSONAL WORK • CREDIT: Javo-Rafakir-JuanJo-Path-
Orbito-1000Changos-DrLatex-Escobas • YEAR: 2005

PLAYER: Fernando Leal
TEAM: Brazil
WWW.FLEAL.COM • FERNANDO@FLEAL.COM
NUMBER: 117
CLIENT: MTV BRASIL • YEAR: 2006 • INFOS: Logo for MTV
BRASIL'S ANNUAL CELEBRITY FOOTBALL CUP

PLAYER: Flavio Bagioli
TEAM: Chile
WWW.DESORG.CL • INFO@DESORG.CL
NUMBER: 40
CLIENT: PERSONAL WORK • YEAR: 2006

PLAYER: Fósforo
TEAM: Spain
WWW.FOSFORO.ES • FOSFORO@FOSFORO.ES
ARTWORKS
NUMBER: 74
CLIENT: PERSONAL WORK • YEAR: 2006 • DESIGNER: Eduardo
Bertone

PLAYER: Freestyle collective
TEAM: USA
WWW.FREESTYLECOLLECTIVE.COM • VICTOR@FREESTYLECOLLEC-
IVE.COM
FREESTYLE COLLECTIVE IS A COLLABORATIVE DESIGN AND
PRODUCTION STUDIO RECOGNIZED FOR ITS UNIQUE ARTISTIC
SENSIBILITY. SPECIALIZING IN EXPLORATORY AND EXPERIMENTAL
DESIGN, FREESTYLE COLLECTIVE DELIVERS CREATIVE ADVERTISING,
PROMOTION AND BRANDING SOLUTIONS TO A BROAD RANGE OF
COMMERCIAL, BROADCAST AND CORPORATE CLIENTS.
NUMBER: 40, 41
CLIENT: PERSONAL WORK • YEAR: 2005 • DESIGNER: Juan Delcan

PLAYER: Gianni Rossi
TEAM: Italy
WWW.GIANNIROSSI.NET • CONTACT@GIANNIROSSI.NET
MY DESIGN WORKS CONSISTS MOSTLY IN PRINT MATERIAL WITH
RANGE OF LOGOTYPES, CORPORATE IDENTITIES, ADS, BOOKS/
REVIEWS, CD/LP COVERS, MOVIE POSTERS... ALSO GRAPHICS FOR
APPAREL, WEB SITES AND CHARACTERS.
NUMBER: 66, 67
CLIENT: PERSONAL WORK • YEAR: 2006 • INFOS: I WANTED TO
TRANSMIT ABOUT THE UNION OF THE WORLD, IN THIS CHAMPION
SHIP IN GERMANY THERE ARE 32 COUNTRY THAT PLAY TOGETHER.
I DESIGNED ALL THE OFFICIAL UNIFORMS AND CHARACTERS...

PLAYER: Henry Obasi | Ppaint
TEAM: United Kingdom
WWW.UNIT.NL • INFO@PPAINT.NET • INFO@UNIT.NL
NUMBER: 76
CLIENT: MOTHER • ILLUSTRATOR: Henry Obasi (ppaint), ART
DIRECTION: Stuart Outhwaite @ MOTHER • YEAR: 2004 INFO:
Commissioned by MOTHER, Press advertising campaign of
A FAN SUPPORTING HIS BELOVED BOLTON WANDERERS. BOLTON
WANDERERS TEAM AS SUPER HEROES TRAINING.

PLAYER: Hideaki Komiyama | TGB des.
TEAM: Japan
WWW.TGBDESIGN.COM • INFO@TGBDESIGN.COM
NUMBER: 16
CLIENT: BUNGEISHUNJU • YEAR: 2005 • ILLUSTRATION BY Ken
Hamaguchi • INFOS: ART DIRECTION WORK FOR "NUMBER"
MAGAZINE BRASIL NATIONAL TEAM
NUMBER: 61
CLIENT: BUNGEISHUNJU • YEAR: 2002 • INFOS: Cover Photo
FOR "NUMBER" MAGAZINE FIFA WORLDCUP 2002 KOREA/JAPAN:
32TEAMS UNIFORM ON JUMBO LEGO.
NUMBER: 117
CLIENT: JAZZY DEPORTISTAS • YEAR: 2005 • INFOS: Music +
FOOTBALL EVENT "KEL" LOGO MARK
NUMBER: 126
CLIENT: 2000BLACK • YEAR: 2002 • INFOS: Booklet page from
Music CD+LP [2000BLACK presents GOOD GOOD vol.2]

PLAYER: Hiroyuki Watanabe
TEAM: Japan
WWW.GEOCITIES.JP/VERSIONFLOWER • W2626H@YBB.NE.JP
GRAPHIC DESIGNER, PAINTER
NUMBER: 44
CLIENT: PERSONAL WORK • YEAR: 2005 • INFOS: THE SCENERY
SERIES COMPUTER GRAPHICS

PLAYER: Hort
TEAM: Germany
WWW.HORT.ORG.UK • WE@HORT.ORG.UK
NUMBER: 128
CLIENT: PERSONAL WORK • YEAR: 2006 • INFO: Poster for
"BOLZEN" MAGAZINE, WWW.BOLZEN-ONLINE.DE/BOLZEN/MAGAZIN

PLAYER: Iaah | Nessim Higson
TEAM: Australia
WWW.IAMALWAYSHUNGRY.COM • NESS@IAMALWAYSHUNGRY.COM
NUMBER: 54
CLIENT: PERSONAL WORK • YEAR: 2006

PLAYER: Inksurge
TEAM: Philippines
WWW.INKSURGE.COM • BROADCAST@INKSURGE.COM
BREWED IN MANILA, PHILIPPINES IN 2002. COFFEE JUNKIES Joyce
AND Rex FOUNDED INKSURGE AS A STIMULANT TO EXERCISE THEIR
CREATIVE DRIVE AND AN EXCUSE FOR WAKING UP LATE. THE BARISTAS
WERE SUMMONED BY Kaldi OF CAFFA ETHOPIA TO HYPERACTIVELY
JOIN IN THE DESIGN WORLD.
NUMBER: 32, 33
CLIENT: PERSONAL WORK • YEAR: 2006

PLAYER: Iván Solbes
TEAM: Spain
WWW.IVANSOLBES.COM • IVAN@IVANSOLBES.COM
IVÁN SOLBES ES UN ILUSTRADOR ESPAÑOL QUE TRABAJA PARA
EL MUNDO DE LA PUBLICIDAD HACIENDO DIBUJOS E INVENTANDO
CAMPAÑAS. COLABORA TAMBIÉN CON EDITORIALES Y PRENSA.
NUMBER: 12, 13
CLIENT: AMENA • YEAR: 2003 • INFO: Posters para una
COMPAÑÍA TELEFÓNICA ESPAÑOLA.

PLAYER: Ippei Gyoubu
TEAM: Japan
WWW.GYOUBU.COM • MAIL@GYOUBU.COM
I AM AN ILLUSTRATOR OF FREE-LANCE IN JAPAN.
NUMBER: 64, 65
CLIENT: ADIDAS JAPAN • YEAR: 2002

PLAYER: Jan Langela
TEAM: Germany
WWW.JANLANGELA.DE • MAIL@JANLANGELA.DE
NUMBER: 120 – 123
CLIENT: PERSONAL WORK • YEAR: 2006

PLAYER: Jeremyville
TEAM: Australia
WWW.JEREMYVILLE.COM • JEREMY@JEREMYVILLE.COM
JEREMYVILLE DESIGNS TOYS, PRODUCES BOOKS SUCH AS Vinyl
Will Kill, COLLABORATIVE PROJECTS SUCH AS Sketchel, AND
CREATES APPAREL AND PRODUCTS SOLD IN STORES LIKE Colette
IN PARIS. HE ALSO CREATES ANIMATIONS OF HIS CHARACTERS FOR
COMPANIES SUCH AS MTV.
NUMBER: 58
CLIENT: PERSONAL WORK • YEAR: 2006
NUMBER: 59
CLIENT: Don't Panic UK & Australia • YEAR: 2006 • INFOS: A2
POSTER DESIGN FOR Don't Panic UK AND Australia

PLAYER: JR
TEAM: France
WWW.JR-ART.NET • JR.EXPO2RUE@GMAIL.COM
JR IS AN STREET ARTIST PHOTOGRAPH WHO REPAST HIS PICTURES
ON THE WALL AROUND THE WORLD. HE PUBLISHED RECENTLY
"CARNET DE RUE" ("MY STREET JOURNAL") PUBLISHER Free presse
(FRANCE)
NUMBER: 112, 113
CREDIT: New-York (Manhattan Mid Packing)

PLAYER: Julia Pfaller
TEAM: Germany
WWW.JULIAPFALLER.DE • JP@JULIAPFALLER.DE
ILLUSTRATOR
NUMBER: 46
CLIENT: die zeit LEBEN • CREDIT: Julia Pfaller, Michael Biedo-
wicz, Katja Kollmann • YEAR: 2005 • DESIGNER: Julia Pfaller
• INFOS: "WÜNSCHE ZUR RETTUNG DER WELT"

PLAYER: Kanardo
TEAM: France
WWW.KANARDO.COM • CONTACT@KANARDO.COM
A TWO HEADED UNIT FOR GRAPHIC DESIGN, CONTEMPORARY
PHOTOGRAPHY, MAGAZINES LAYOUT AND UNEXPECTED PROJECTS.
NUMBER: 56
CLIENT: PERSONAL WORK • YEAR: 2005

PLAYER: Karoly Kiralyfalvi |
Extraverage Productions
TEAM: Hungary
WWW.EXTRAVERAGE.NET • WWW.DREZIGN.HU •
DREZ@EXTRAVERAGE.NET
NUMBER: 96
CLIENT: PERSONAL WORK • YEAR: 2006

PLAYER: KesselsKramer
TEAM: Netherlands
WWW.KESSELSKRAMER.COM • CHURCH@KESSELSKRAMER.NL
KESSELSKRAMER IS A CREATIVE COMMUNICATIONS COMPANY
LOCATED IN AMSTERDAM AND IS RESPONSIBLE FOR CAMPAIGNS
RANGING FROM Diesel, The Hans Brinker Budget Hotel
Amsterdam, Ben Mobile Communications AS WELL AS PROD-
UCT INNOVATIONS, NEW BRANDS AND A DOCUMENTARY
FILM TITLED "The Other Final."
NUMBER: 82
CLIENT: Vrij Nederland • CREDIT: KesselsKramer • YEAR:
1996 • DESIGNER: Erik Kessels, Johan Kramer • INFOS: Holy
Grounds AN EDITORIAL PROJECT FOR THE 1996 EUROPEAN CUP,
HOLY GROUNDS INCLUDES 1-TO-1 PHOTOGRAPHS OF THE FAMOUS
FOOTBALL PITCHES IN BRITAIN WHERE THE TOURNAMENT WAS TO
BE PLAYED.
NUMBER: 102
CLIENT: Het Parool • YEAR: 1998 • DESIGNER: Erik Kessels,
Johan Kramer • INFOS: Poster campaign – A POSTER CAMPAIGN
FOR THE AMSTERDAM NEWSPAPER ANNOUNCING ITS DEDICATED
COVERAGE OF THE COMING WORLD CUP IN FRANCE. POSTERS
FEATURE READERS OF Het Parool WITH A SPECIALLY MADE FOOT-
BALL CONSTRUCTED OF THE VERY MATERIAL OF THE NEWSPAPER.

NUMBER: 103
CLIENT: HARD GRAS MAGAZINE • YEAR: 1998 Ü DESIGNER: ERIK KESSELS, JOHAN KRAMER • INFOS: POSTER – A POSTER FOR THE FOOTBALL LOVER'S MAGAZINE HARD GRAS NUMBER 14 FEATURES AN OLD, HISTORICAL IMAGE OF A DUTCH FOOTBALL PLAYER IN THE CLASSIC NATIONAL KIT, HOLDING THE LATEST ISSUE OF THE MAGAZINE.
NUMBER: 104
CLIENT: DUTCH MAGAZINE • YEAR: 1997 • DESIGNER: ERIK KESSELS, JOHAN KRAMER • INFOS: EDITORIAL – THE EDITORIAL FOCUSES ON THE QUESTION "WHERE ARE THEY NOW?" USING OLD FOOTBALL CARDS AND ACTUAL PHOTOS OF THE FORMER PLAYERS.
NUMBER: 105
CLIENT: HET PAROOL • YEAR: 2000 • DESIGNER: ERIK KESSELS, JOHAN KRAMER • INFOS: BOOKLET – PORTRAITS OF FOOTBALL FANS FROM DIFFERENT COUNTRIES LIVING IN AMSTERDAM. EACH FAN IS INTERVIEWED AND PHOTOGRAPHED WEARING THE SHIRT OF THEIR HOME COUNTRY AND THEIR NATIONAL TEAM IN THEIR LOCAL NEIGHBOURHOODS OF AMSTERDAM.
NUMBER: 107
CLIENT: NIKE • CREDIT: © NIKE • YEAR: 1996 • DESIGNER: ERIK KESSELS, JOHAN KRAMER • INFOS: TAKING THE INITIATIVE FROM FOOTBALL-CRAZY KIDS LIVING IN URBAN AREAS THAT LACK GREEN SPACES, NIKE IS NOW ABLE TO SUPPLY TEMPORARY GOALS ON WALLS THAT ARE SUITABLE FOR PLAY.
NUMBER: 108, 109
CLIENT: HET PAROOL • YEAR: 1998 • DESIGNER: ERIK KESSELS INFOS: ART PROJECT – JULIAN GERMAIN DEVELOPED AND EXECUTED AN ART PROJECT AND BOOK TITLED ‚NO MUNDO MARAVILHOSO DO FUTEBOL' CREATED IN THE CITY OF BELO HORIZONTE, BRAZIL WHICH CHRONICLES LIFE AND FOOTBALL. CHILDREN IN BELO HORIZONTE WERE GIVEN CAMERAS AND ASKED TO PHOTOGRAPH WHAT FOOTBALL MEANS TO THEM.
NUMBER: 110, 111
CLIENT: SELF INITIATED PROJECT BY KESSELSKRAMER • YEAR: 2002 • DESIGNER: MATTHIJS DE JONGH, JOHAN KRAMER • INFOS: THE OTHER FINAL (DOCUMENTARY + BOOK TITLE) - A CULTURAL EVENT, BOOK AND DOCUMENTARY ABOUT THE MATCH PLAYED BY THE WORLD'S TWO LOWESTRANKED FOOTBALL TEAMS. BHUTAN AND MONTSERRAT WERE ASKED TO PARTICIPATE ON THE SAME DAY AS THE WORLD CUP FINAL IN JAPAN IN 2002. THE MATCH WAS PLAYED ON JUNE 30, 2002 IN THIMPU, BHUTAN AT THE FOOTSTEPS OF THE HIMALAYAS. THERE WAS NO WINNER OR LOSER AS THE MATCH WAS IN THE SPIRIT OF FRIENDSHIP AND CULTURAL UNDERSTANDING, DEMONSTRATING THAT FOOTBALL CAN BE PLAYED FOR FAR MORE THAN MONETARY REWARD AND PERSONAL FAME. THE BOOK CONTAINS PHOTOGRAPHS BY HANS VAN DER MEER, THAT DOCUMENTS THE MATCH BETWEEN BHUTAN AND MONTSERRAT.
NUMBER: 125
CLIENT: FC WALVISCH • YEAR: 2003 • DESIGNER: KAREN HEUTER, JOHAN KRAMER • INFOS: FC WALVISCH (IDENTITY) - COMBINING THE MUSICAL PASSION WITH THE FOOTBALL PASSION OF A SOUND STUDIO OWNER, THIS HOUSESTYLE MIXES IMAGES OF OLD FOOTBALL PLAYERS AND CLUBS INTO A MUSICAL FOOTBALL CLUB CALLED FC WALVISCH.
NUMBER: 133
CLIENT: DO (A KESSELSKRAMER INITIATIVE) • YEAR: 2002 • DESIGNER: MARTI GUIXE • INFOS: DO FC - A DO PROJECT COLLABORATION WITH DESIGNER MARTI GUIXE CALLED DO FC PROVIDES FOOTBALL FANS WITH ALL THE EQUIPMENT NECESSARY FOR STARTING A FOOTBALL CLUB IN THE FORM OF TAPE ROLLS. THE KIT COMES IN A HANDY CARDBOARD BAG AND INCLUDES ROLLS OF TAPE FOR NAME BADGES, PITCH LINES, FANS, TROPHIES AND, OF COURSE, THE FOOTBALL. THE MESSAGE OF DO FC IS TO REMIND FANS ABOUT THE SIMPLICITY OF THE GAME DURING THE TIME OF THE WORLD CUP IN JAPAN. DO FC EXHIBITED AND WAS FOR SALE IN TOKYO DURING THE WORLD CUP.

PLAYER: KEV SPECK
TEAM: UNITED KINGDOM
WWW.KEVSPECK.COM
NUMBER: 88
CLIENT: PERSONAL WORK

PLAYER: KIMERA
TEAM: MEXICO
WWW.KIMERA.COM.MX • GABRIEL@KIMERA.COM.MX
KIMERA IS A GRAPHIC, TYPOGRAPHIC AND ILLUSTRATION STUDIO BASED IN MEXICO CITY SINCE 1994. GABRIEL MARTÍNEZ MEAVE IS PRINCIPAL AND FOUNDER OF KIMERA. SOME OF HIS ORIGINAL FONTS ARE DISTRIBUTED WORLDWIDE BY ADOBE SYSTEMS.

NUMBER: 90
CLIENT: PERSONAL WORK • YEAR: 2005–2006 • INFO: ILLUSTRATION AND ORIGINAL TYPEFACES AZTLAN AND NEOCODEX BY GABRIEL MARTÍNEZ MEAVE. AN AZTEC-INSPIRED POSTER FEATURING FUTBOLTECATL-PAMBOLTEOTL, GOD OF FOOTBALL. ILLUSTRATED ON THE TRADITION OF ANCIENT MEXICAN TLACUILOS, OR SCRIBES, TRANSLATED INTO THE DIGITAL REALM.

PLAYER: KLEIN DYTHAM ARCHITECTURE
TEAM: JAPAN
WWW.KLEIN-DYTHAM.COM • KDA@KLEIN-DYTHAM.COM
NUMBER: 115
CLIENT: ADIDAS • YEAR: 2003 • ADVERTISING DESIGN: TBWA / TOKYO • STREET MAP / PLANT FLOWER GRAPHICS: NAMAIKI + SUPERFUTURE • INFO: GREEN GREEN SCREEN IS A LIVE, GROWING CONSTRUCTION SCREEN 274 METERS LONG, RUNNING ALMOST THE FULL LENGTH OF TOKYO'S VERSION OF THE CHAMPS ELYSEES, OMOTESANDO. THE SCREEN WAS IN PLACE FOR 3 YEARS. THERE ARE 13 TYPES OF EVERGREEN PLANTS THAT FORM A PATTERN OF STRIPES, SIMILIAR TO A BARCODE, THAT GREW AND MATURED OVER THE 3 YEARS. A VARIETY OF GRAPHIC WALLPAPERS ON THE THEME OF PLANTS WAS INTERSPERSED AMONG THE REAL GREENS.

PLAYER: LEON VYMENETS
TEAM: CANADA
WWW.STEREO-EROS.COM • LEON@STEREO-EROS.COM
LEON CREATES ART THAT FLOWS WITH HIS LIFE'S MANTRA OF SIMPLICITY, MINIMALISM AND A SENSE OF CHILDLIKE ADVENTURE. HIS ILLUSTRATIONS AND DRAWINGS ARE TIGHTLY PACKAGED, YET SPONTANEOUS AND RAW. INSPIRED BY URBAN CULTURE, LEON'S WORK IS A COMBINATION OF UNCONSTRAINED IDEAS THAT ARE MOLDED BY REFLECTIONS OF THE PAST AND PRESENT. LEON IS WORKING IN TORONTO AS A FREELANCE ARTIST.
NUMBER: 89
CLIENT: PERSONAL WORK • YEAR: 2005/2006 • CREDIT: ROMAN ABRAMOVICH

PLAYER: LOLO
TEAM: SPAIN
LOLO2077@YAHOO.COM
NUMBER: 85
CLIENT: PERSONAL WORK • YEAR: 2006

PLAYER: LINDEDESIGN |
CHRISTIAN LINDEMANN
TEAM: GERMANY
WWW.LINDEDESIGN.DE • INFO@LINDEDESIGN.DE
NUMBER: 57
CLIENT: PERSONAL WORK • YEAR: 2006

PLAYER: MASA
TEAM: VENEZUELA
WWW.MASA.COM.VE • INFO@MASA.COM.VE
ART DIRECTION, DESIGN/ILLUSTRATION AND MOTION GRAPHICS FOR ENTERTAINMENT, MUSIC, FASHION AND URBAN/YOUTH ORIENTED CULTURE RELATED CLIENTS. MASA'S WORK HAS A STRONG EMPHASIS IN THE RESEARCH OF LATIN AMERICAN POP AND WORLD WIDE CONTEMPORARY STREET CULTURE FORMS AND IDEAS TO ADD AND PRODUCE A CROSSOVER WITH DISTINCTIVE RESULT IN EVERY WORK. DELIVERING FRESH IDEAS AND STRONG BRAND IDENTITIES THAT HAS ATTRACTED INTERNATIONAL CLIENTS BY MIXING LATIN AMERICAN COLOURS AND FORMS WITH AN EUROPEAN BLEND.
NUMBER: 50, 51
CLIENT: PERSONAL WORK • YEAR: 2006

PLAYER: MATTHIAS GEPHART
TEAM: GERMANY
WWW.DISTURBANITY.COM • INFO@DISTURBANITY.COM
DISTURBANITY IS A ONE-MAN-DEPARTMENT FOR GRAPHIC TREATMENT AND ILLUSTRATION. CURRENTLY LOCATED IN THE CENTRAL RUHR AREA OF WEST GERMANY, MATTHIAS GEPHARTS STUDIO IS WORKING HARD ON DEVELOPING WEIRD AND ROUGH STUFF, NO MATTER IF FOR ARTISTIC OR COMMERCIAL NEEDS.
NUMBER: 49
CLIENT: FOOTBALL-FANS • YEAR: 2006 • INFOS: JUST ANOTHER PIECE OF THE CAMPAIGN – WHAT DOES IT ACTUALLY TELL US? IT'S NOT QUITE OBVIOUS, BUT THINKING ABOUT IT SURELY MAKES MORE SENSE THAN SHOUTING OUT SOME NONSENSE IN YOUR LOCAL ARENA, WHILE THOUSAND OF OTHER FREAKS DO NOTHING BUT THE SAME.

PLAYER: MITCH PAONE
TEAM: USA
WWW.DREAMERSINKAESTHETICS.NET • MITCH@DREAMERSINKAESTHETICS.NET
NUMBER: 26, 27
CLIENT: PERSONAL WORK • YEAR: 2006 • INFOS: HOOLIGAN UNITED MOTO, HOOLIGAN UNITED ELK SEAL

PLAYER: MIXKO
TEAM: UNITED KINGDOM
WWW.MIXKO.NET • INFO@MIXKO.NET
10 METERS SWIMMERS BADGE 1987
NUMBER: 130, 131
CLIENT: PERSONAL WORK • CREDIT: COPYRIGHT © 2006. ALEX GARNETT, MIXKO. ALL RIGHTS RESERVED. • YEAR: 2005, 2006 • DESIGNER: ALEX GARNETT • INFOS: "THE FINAL WHISTLE". 1:18 SCALE, STAINLESS STEEL WHISTLE CHAIR/SCULPTURE; "GOAL" CELEBRATION SHIRT. A PLAIN T-SHIRT WITH A HIDDEN SURPRISE FOR EXCITING GOAL CELEBRATIONS; "BALL WALLET". A DISTINCTIVE WALLET MADE FROM FOOTBALL PATCHES. AVAILABLE IN 2 STYLES; FLAT (PICTURED) AND CURVED – TO FIT MORE COMFORTABLY IN YOUR BACK POCKET; "MATS OF THE DAY". A SET OF HEXAGONAL BEER MATS, WHICH CREATE A FOOTBALL GRAPHIC ON YOUR TABLE; "FOOTBOWL". A CERAMIC FRUIT BOWL, SLIP CAST FROM A DEFLATED FOOTBALL.

PLAYER: NATSUKI LEE
TEAM: JAPAN
WWW.DIGMEOUT.NET/LEE
NUMBER: 28
CLIENT: MDN CORPORATION • ART DIRECTOR: MITSUNOBU HOSOYAMADA • YEAR: 2004 • TITLE: "FIRE OF SOUL"

PLAYER: NORDPOL
TEAM: DEUTSCHLAND
WWW.NORDPOL.COM • HALLO@NORDPOL.COM
NUMBER: 8, 9
CLIENT: ALTONA 93 • YEAR: 2002 • CREATIVE DIRECTOR: LARS RÜHMANN, ART DIRECTOR: BJÖRN RÜHMANN, BERTRAND KIRSCHENHOFER, GRAPHICS: KRISTOFFER HEILEMANN, BJÖRN RÜHMANN, BERTRAND KIRSCHENHOFER, TEXT: INGMAR BARTELS • INFO: IMAGE CAMPAIGN FOR THE GERMAN 4TH LEAGUE AMATEUR TEAM OF "ALTONA 93", HAMBURG, PLAYING WITH WORDS AND OVERSTYLED IMAGES OF THE PLAYERS.

PLAYER: PUMA PAINTURA PROJECT
WWW.PUMA.COM
NUMBER: 134 - 137
YEAR: 2005 • CURATED BY TOMOMI NAKAJIMA, STOIQUE (JAPAN), WWW.STOIQUE.NET FOR PUMA • ARTISTS: BEN DRURY, KOSTAS SEREMETIS, DAVID FOLDVARI, KATE GIBB, GENTA KOSUMI, VÅR, REGGIE PEDRO, MR. JAGO, STEFF PLAETZ, WILL BARRAS, REAS, ESPO

PLAYER: PATRICIO OLIVER
TEAM: ARGENTINA
WWW.PATRICIOOLIVER.COM.AR • PATRICIOOLIVER@GMAIL.COM
NUMBER: 75
CLIENT: PERSONAL WORK • YEAR: 2005

PLAYER: PANTIESTUDIO
TEAM: MEXICO
WWW.PANTIESTUDIO.COM • CONTACTO@PANTIESTUDIO.COM
COMMUNICATIONS SOLUTIONS. DESIGN AND ADVERTISING
NUMBER: 45
CLIENT: PERSONAL WORK • YEAR: 2005 • CREDIT: CEJAS • DESIGNER: JORGE CEJUDO • TITLE: DEFENSE
NUMBER: 78
CLIENT: PERSONAL WORK • YEAR: 2005 • CREDIT: CEJAS • DESIGNER: JORGE CEJUDO • TITLE: STRATEGY "03"
NUMBER: 79
CLIENT: PERSONAL WORK • YEAR: 1998 • CREDIT: CEJAS • DESIGNER: JORGE CEJUDO • TITLES: WORDIMAGE, "1_2_1998"

PLAYER: Pfadfinderei
TEAM: GERMANY
WW.PFADFINDEREI.COM • ZELT@PFADFINDEREI.COM
CLIENT: ADIDAS • YEAR: 2003/2004 • INFO: TRAINER: OPENED
ND CLOSED BY USING THE PAPER-LACES; FOLLOW-UP PROMOTIONAL
ECES TO THE ADIDAS-SHOWS 2003 AND 2004; BOTH PACKAGES
ERE DESIGNED TO BE MADE FROM ONE PIECE OF PAPER; LIMITED
O 15 PIECES, HAND-CUT AND HAND-ASSEMBLED AT PFADFINDEREI •
VD-PRODUCTION: PFADFINDEREI

PLAYER: PIETARI POSTI
TEAM: FINLAND
WW.PIETARIPOSTI.COM • PIETARI.POSTI@GMAIL.COM
IETARI POSTI IS A FINNISH FREELANCER ILLUSTRATOR LIVING AND
ORKING IN BARCELONA, SPAIN.
NUMBER: 77
CLIENT: PERSONAL WORK • YEAR: 2006 • TITLE: THE BANANA KICK

PLAYER: RAPHAZEN
TEAM: JAPAN
TTP://RAPHAZEN.COM • INFO@RAPHAZEN.COM
NUMBER: 119
CLIENT: PERSONAL WORK • YEAR: 2006 • DESIGNER: SHINSUKE
AMADYA AND SHU THE S.L • TITLES: EXAMINATION OF VISUAL
CUITYI, RYU_SENI, RYU_SEN2

PLAYER: REGINA
TEAM: JAPAN
WW.REPUBLICOFREGINA.COM
NUMBER: 24
CLIENT: PERSONAL WORK • YEAR: 2006 • TITLE: "RONALDO DE
SSIS MOREIRA"

PLAYER: ROB HARE
TEAM: UNITED KINGDOM
W.ROBHARE.CO.UK • ROB@ROBHARE.CO.UK
O-FOUNDER OF BWB DESIGN COLLECTIVE ROB HARE, IS A LONDON
ASED FREELANCE ILLUSTRATOR. HE HAS PRODUCED ARTWORK
R A WIDE RANGE OF CREATIVE CORNERS INCLUDING EDITORIAL,
DVERTISING CAMPAIGNS AND DESIGNER FASHION COLLECTIONS.
OB HARE AIMS TO BRING REFRESHING AND VIBRANT COLOUR TO A
X OF VECTOR SHAPES, PAINTED BRUSH STROKES AND PHOTO-
RAPHIC TEXTURES.
NUMBER: 47, 93
LIENT: PERSONAL WORK • YEAR: 2006

PLAYER: SAMMY STEIN
TEAM: FRANCE
AMMYSZX@GMAIL.COM
RTIST/ILLUSTRATOR/GRAPHISTE
NUMBER: 118
LIENT: PERSONAL WORK • YEAR: 2006

PLAYER: SEMITRANSPARENT DESIGN
TEAM: JAPAN
WW.SEMITRANSPARENTDESIGN.COM • INFO@SEMITRANSPARENT-
ESIGN.COM
NUMBER: 5
LIENT: PERSONAL WORK • YEAR: 2006

PLAYER: SOAP CREATIVE
TEAM: AUSTRALIA
WW.SOAP.COM.AU • BIZ@SOAP.COM.AU
OUNDED IN 2002, SOAP IS AN ONLINE CREATIVE AGENCY. OUR
ECIALISATION IS THE CONCEPTING, DESIGN AND DEVELOPMENT OF
TERACTIVE WEBSITES, GAMES AND ONLINE MEDIA FOR ADVERTIS-
G AND MARKETING BASED CAMPAIGNS.
NUMBER: 52, 53
LIENT: FOOTBALL FEDERATION AUSTRALIA • CREDIT: PROJECT
ANAGER: LISA MAIN / MIXED INDUSTRY • YEAR: 2005 •
ESIGNER: CHRISTIAN LAYUGAN / SOAP CREATIVE • INFOS: THIS
TWORK ACCOMPANIED A NEW TVC BEING UNVEILED AT THE
UNCH PARTY OF THE NEW AUSTRALIAN A-LEAGUE IN 2005. THE
OJECT INCLUDED A 3 MINUTE MOTION PIECE THAT LOOPED ON
ASMA SCREENS DURING THE EVENT, TWO LARGE FEATURE WALLS,
NNERS AND A SERIES OF IMAGES PROJECTED ONTO THE WALLS
THE INTERIOR AND EXTERIOR. THE STENCIL/STREET LOOK WAS
SIGNED TO TIE IN WITH A TEASER CAMPAIGN LEADING UP TO THE
UNCH.

PLAYER: STEPHANE MANEL
TEAM: FRANCE
WWW.STEPHANEMANEL.COM • INFO@STEPHANEMANEL.COM
NUMBER: 92
CLIENT: PERSONAL WORK • YEAR: 2006 • INFO: "GEORGE BEST",
PUBLISHED IN TOKION, MARCH 2006. NEW YORK, USA.
NUMBER: 94
YEAR: 2006 • INFO: FROM THE "MONDIAL 2006" BOOK PUBLISHED
BY LE BARON PERCHÉ. FRANCE, 2006 - FROM THE "MAKE MY DAY"
SERIE ON WWW.STEPHANEMANEL.COM
NUMBER: 95
YEAR: 2006 • COVER FOR THE "MONDIAL 2006" BOOK. BY
M.BONNAMY, C.GHEMMOUR, N.MABROUK, F.SANCHEZ AND
P-E.MINONZIO ILLUSTRATIONS BY STEPHANE MANEL, PUBLISHED BY
LE BARON PERCHÉ. FRANCE, 2006

PLAYER: SUNDAY-VISION
TEAM: JAPAN
WWW.SUNDAY-VISION.COM • INFO@SUNDAY-VISION.COM
NUMBER: 86
CLIENT: PERSONAL WORK • YEAR: 2002 • DESIGNER: SHINSUKE
KOSHIO / SUNDAY-VISION
NUMBER: 117
CLIENT: PERSONAL WORK • YEAR: 2003 • DESIGNER: SHINSUKE
KOSHIO), ATSUSHI AOKI (ADD) • TITLE: SWITCH STANCE & ADD
FOOTBALL FONT [FOOTBALL IS OUR LANGUAGE]
NUMBER: 117, 144
CLIENT: SOPH.CO., LTD • YEAR: 2002 • DESIGNER: SHINSUKE
KOSHIO / SUNDAY-VISION

PLAYER: SUPEREXPRESSO
TEAM: ITALY
WWW.SUPEREXPRESSO.COM • MIKE@SUPEREXPRESSO.COM
SUPEREXPRESSO IS ROBOTS AND DUST. LET MACHINES SPREAD THE
LOVE. PUSH THE GREEN BUTTON! BLACK COFFEE WITH NO SUGAR,
PLEASE.
NUMBER: 30
CLIENT: PERSONAL WORK • YEAR: 2006 • DESIGNER: MICHELE
ANGELO • INFO: SWEAT-INTEREST IN CONFLICT-SOUL-PRIDE

PLAYER: THE BANG - BILL DOUGLAS
TEAM: CANADA
WWW.COUPE-MAG.COM • THEBANG@BELLNET.CA
BILL DOUGLAS IS THE FOUNDER OF THE BANG, A MULTI-DISCIPLI-
NARY STUDIO SPECIALIZING IN BOOK AND PUBLICATION DESIGN.
OVER THE PAST DECADE DOUGLAS HAS CREATED OVER 400 JACKET
AND BOOK DESIGNS FOR A MULTITUDE OF PUBLISHERS INCLUDING
HOUSE OF ANANSI, DOUBLEDAY,
NUMBER: 37
CLIENT: PERSONAL WORK • YEAR: 2005 • INFOS: GEORGE BEST
POSTERS

PLAYER: TOAN VU-HUU
TEAM: FRANCE
WWW.TOANVUHUU.COM • ME@TOANVUHUU.COM
VISUAL CONCEPTION, CORPORATE IDENTITY, SIGNAGE SYSTEMS
NUMBER: 10
CLIENT: PERSONAL WORK • YEAR: 2006 • INFOS: UNIVERSAL GOAL

PLAYER: TOKIDOKI | SIMONE LEGNO
TEAM: ITALY
WWW.TOKIDOKI.IT • SIMONE@TOKIDOKI.IT
2004: MOVED TO LOS ANGELES TO DEVELOP MY OWN TOKIDOKI
APPAREL AND ART LICENSING BRAND WITH 2 BUSINESS PARTNERS.
JUST LAUNCHED ON THE MARKET THE FIRST TEE SHIRT LINE, START-
ING FROM CALIFORNIA AND SPREADING AROUND THE WORLD ON
OTHER ITEMS LIKE VINYL TOYS WITH STRANGECO AN SF BASED
COMPANY, ART-SKATEBOARD, PIN BADGES AND MORE TO COME.
TOKIDOKI.IT STARTED AS MY PROFESSIONAL PORTFOLIO AND ARTIS-
TIC DIARY WHILE LIVING IN ITALY.
NUMBER: 62, 63
CLIENT: PERSONAL WORK • YEAR: 2006

PLAYER: TOMOKO TSUNEDA
TEAM: JAPAN
WWW2.OCN.NE.JP/~TSUNE/
ILLUSTRATOR
NUMBER: 29
CLIENT: PERSONAL WORK • YEAR: 2005 – 2006

PLAYER: TONIA FRIEDL
TEAM: AUSTRIA
WWW.KLASSEHICKMANN.COM
NUMBER: 130
CLIENT: PERSONAL WORK • YEAR: 2006 • INFOS: STUDENT
PROJECT "TURNIER FÜR ANGEWANDTEN FUSSBALL 2002" AT
UNIVERSITY OF APPLIED ARTS VIENNA, CLASS OF FONS HICKMANN;
2 POSTERS, PLAYING WITH THE SUBJECT "PLAYING FIELD" FOR THE
TOURNAMENT BETWEEN 16 MIXED GENDER TEAMS, HELD IN THE LOFT
OF FONS HICKMANNS CLASS AT THE UNIVERSITY • SUPERVISION:
FONS HICKMANN, KATHARINA USCHAN

PLAYER: TOTUMA
TEAM: VENEZUELA
WWW.TOTUMA.TV • INFO@TOTUMAWEB.COM
NUMBER: 2
CLIENT: PERSONAL WORK • YEAR: 2006 • DESIGNER: MANUEL
PIÑA, CRISTINA BRICEÑO, JORGE VIGAS
NUMBER: 19
CLIENT: PERSONAL WORK • YEAR: 2006 • DESIGNER: PABLO
IRANZO
NUMBER: 70
CLIENT: PERSONAL WORK • YEAR: 2006 • DESIGNER: ANDREINA
DIAZ

PLAYER: TSUTOMU UMEZAWA
TEAM: JAPAN
WWW.UMEZAWATSUTOMU.COM • TSUTOMU.UMEZAWA@GMAIL.COM
NUMBER: 114
CLIENT: PERSONAL WORK; A3P (ONLY BIG PHOTO) • YEAR: 2005

PLAYER: TYPEHOLICS
TEAM: GERMANY
HTTP://TYPEHOLICS.COM • CONTACT@TYPEHOLICS.DE
NUMBER: 124
DESIGNER: HENNING WESKAMP

PLAYER: VÅR
TEAM: SWEDEN
WWW.WOO.SE • GRANDIN@WOO.SE
"VÅR" IS A SWEDISH WORD MEANING BOTH "OURS" AND
"SPRINGTIME". IT IS ALSO THE NAME OF DESIGN AND ILLUSTRA-
TION TEAM KARL GRANDIN (AMSTERDAM) AND BJORN KARVESTEDT
(STOCKHOLM). THEY WORK IN A WIDE RANGE OF MEDIA, AND
THEIR DESIGNS HAVE BEEN FEATURED ON BOOK AND ALBUM
COVERS, FABRICS, POSTERS, FURNITURE, WALLS AND IN
MAGAZINES AND FILMS. VÅR HAVE EXHIBITED IN EUROPE, JAPAN
AND THE US.
NUMBER: 138
CLIENT: PAINTURA PITCH PROJECT • YEAR: 2002/2003 • DESIGNER:
VÅR, KARL GRANDIN & BJÖRN ATLDAX

PLAYER: VIAGRAFIK
TEAM: GERMANY
WWW.VIAGRAFIK.COM • MNWRKS@VIAGRAFIK.COM
NUMBER: 117
CLIENT: PERSONAL WORK • YEAR: 2006 • DESIGNER: ANDRÉ
NOSSEK • INFOS: 3D SOCCER MODELING KIT
NUMBER: 127
CLIENT: TRIPLUS CLOTHING • YEAR: 2005 • DESIGNER: LARS HERZIG
• INFOS: SHIRT GRAPHIC

PLAYER: VISUALDATA | RONALD WISSE
TEAM: NETHERLANDS
WWW.VISUALDATA.ORG • VISUALDATA@CHELLO.NL
OUTPUT FOR SCREEN, PRINT, PRODUCT.
NUMBER: 80
CLIENT: PERSONAL WORK • YEAR: 2005 • DESIGNER: RONALD
WISSE

PLAYER: YASUSHI CHO | LAUGHTER
TEAM: JAPAN
WWW5.OCN.NE.JP/~LAUGHTER/ • CHO@HELEN.OCN.NE.JP
YASUSHI CHO IS AN ARTIST WHO MAINLY MAKES THE VISUAL BOOKS
USING PRINTED MATTERS AND PHOTOGRAPHS WITH A PUBLISHER
NAME "LAUGHTER." IT IS THE KEYNOTE TO EXPRESS THINGS CLOSE
TO US IN A FAMILIAR WAY, THE BOOK WORKS ARE PRINTED BY THE
PHOTOCOPY MACHINE AND BO
NUMBER: 38, 39
CLIENT: PERSONAL WORK • YEAR: 2006 • TITLES: SPECTATORS
(COLLAGE), GRASS (COLLAGE), OVERLAP (COLOR SEPARATION,
OVERPRINT)

Play Loud!

Edited by Robert Klanten, Hendrik Hellige, MASA
Project Management: MASA and Hendrik Hellige
Cover layout and illustration: MASA (www.masa.com.ve)
Layout: Hendrik Hellige
Production: Janni Milstrey

Printed by Artes Gráficas Palermo, Madrid

Published by Die Gestalten Verlag, Berlin, 2006
ISBN 3-89955-157-5

Bibliographic information published by Die Deutsche
Bibliothek. Die Deutsche Bibliothek lists this publication in
the Deutsche Nationalbibliografie; detailed bibliographic
data are available in the Internet at http://dnb.ddb.de.

For more information please check: www.die-gestalten.de

Respect copyright, encourage creativity!